A NEW FORAGER'S GUIDE

—— TO ——

WILD FOOD

100 COMMON PLANTS & MUSHROOMS

Easy Identification and Harvest in North America

DENNIS CARSON

For more information, visit the publisher's website at www.offgridlivinghacks.com.

Published by Off Grid Living Hacks

Printed in the United States of America

First Edition: November 2023

ISBN: 978-1-963155-00-6

EXCLUSIVE BONUS: UNLOCK YOUR FORAGING POTENTIAL

Thank you for diving into the world of wild edibles! We're delighted to offer you an exclusive bundle—absolutely FREE!

1. eBook: "Foraging Kitchen: A North American Wild Edibles Cookbook"—Delve into the same 100 wild plants and mushrooms featured in this book, paired with 300+ easy-to-follow and inspirational recipes perfect for home cooking.

2. The Forager's Calendar—a high-resolution PDF guide crafted for foragers like you. This free download is ready for you to print and use on all your foraging adventures, and you'll have the growing seasons of the 100 plants and mushrooms covered in this book at your fingertips.

Don't miss out—**visit the link or scan the QR code below** to claim your exclusive bonus now!

SCAN ME

www.offgridlivinghacks.com/bundle

Plus, you'll get the chance to receive our upcoming books for free and enjoy our latest book deals.

CONTENTS

INTRODUCTION

" Look at the birds of the air;
they do not sow or reap or store
away in barns, and yet your
heavenly Father feeds them.
Are you not much more
valuable than they? "

Matthew 6:26

Imagine living in a world where you have to find your own food every day. That's what our ancestors did for most of human history, until they started farming about 12,000 years ago. They were foraging, which means searching widely for food or provisions. For millions of years, they hunted animals, fished in rivers and oceans, and gathered plants and fruits from the natural environment. They had to be resourceful and adaptable to survive in different conditions and seasons.

In the fast-paced, technology-driven world we live in now, it's easy to forget that food doesn't originate in grocery stores or packaged in boxes. It begins in the wild, and there's a primal satisfaction in sourcing food from nature, just as our ancestors did. Forag-ing not only connects us to our roots but also encourages us to explore, to get our hands dirty, to immerse ourselves in nature and to learn her rhythms and secrets.

The Benefits of Foraging
Superfoods Galore

In the wilderness, you'll find a fresh array of edible plants and mushrooms untouched by genetic modification, pesticides, or her-bicides. It's like an organic farmer's market that's open 24/7, offering nutrient-packed botanicals, freely available to anyone who seeks them out. And there's more to this than meets the eye. According to the Food and Agriculture Organization, these wild foods are remarkably rich in micronutrients, making them excellent contributors to nutritious and balanced diets (FAO, 2019). So why spend on expensive, store-bought "superfoods" when you can forage for nutrient-dense goodies in your backyard?

It's Like Having Nature's Discount Card

Grocery bills have been rising rapidly in recent years, with some food items becoming much more expensive. Foraging can take a load off your grocery budget, providing free food to supplement your daily meals. With some basic foraging skills, walking in your backyard or local park could become a diverse feast. You might question the practicality, but real-world evidence from Australia shows families saving up to $150 a week on groceries by foraging (Swain, 2023). As you explore North American terrain, you might find similar opportunities to save, making each foray into nature feel like cashing in on a discount card.

Because Who Wants to Be Hangry in the Wild

Survival skills aren't just for Bear Grylls wannabes. Foraging is as essential as knowing how to make a fire or build a shelter, providing sustenance when the chips are down. It could mean the difference between life and death in certain situations, as it did for Amanda Eller, a yoga instructor and hiker who survived 17 days in the Hawaiian wilderness by foraging for wild foods, including strawberry guavas. She was eventually found by a search and rescue team (Kerr, 2019).

Your Rainy Day Food Insurance

Foraging can be an invaluable strategy for ensuring food security during scarcity. History has shown that wild foods like berries, nuts, and roots can be more abundant and accessible than cultivated crops, particularly during drought or other natural disasters. For example, during World War II, many families turned to foraging due to rationing restrictions. Foraging provided nourishment and relief for those stranded in the disaster-stricken area.

Eating Green, Literally and Figuratively

Foraging is essentially nature's version of zero-waste grocery shopping. It eliminates the energy-intensive transportation and packaging involved in conventional food production and supports the preservation of local ecosystems. By foraging, we feed ourselves and help maintain the balance in our environment. Ethical foraging can provide food while enhancing the diversity and abundance of plants and animals in rural landscapes.

Forage Your Way to Fitness

Think of foraging as the world's most natural gym membership. There's walking, hiking, and even the occasional climb, all while you hunt for your next meal. But it's not just physical; the sense of accomplishment when you uncover an array of edible flowers, berries, nuts, and leafy greens is unbeatable. Plus, the focus on nature helps reduce stress and boost well-being.

In this chapter, we've explored the extensive benefits of foraging - far more than just the excitement of discovering free food. We've started our journey towards self-sufficiency and sustainability, all provided by the natural world.

References:

Food and Agriculture Organization. (2019). State of biodiversity for food and agriculture. https://www.fao.org/state-of-biodiversity-for-food-agriculture/en/

Swain, S. (2023). Aussie families save on groceries by foraging for food. 9News.com.au. https://www.9news.com.au/national/australian-families-saving-money-on-groceries-by-foraging-tips-to-save-money/d61871fe-716d-495c-b50d-b6a78651cd72.

Kerr, B. (2019, May 25). Amanda Eller, Hiker Lost in Hawaii Forest, Is Found Alive After 17 Days. The New York Times. https://www.nytimes.com/2019/05/25/us/hawaii-hiker.html

FORAGING 101

" *Study nature, love nature,*
stay close to nature.
It will never fail you. "

Frank Lloyd Wright

Embarking on the adventure of foraging can be both rewarding and fulfilling. This chapter propels you into that journey, starting with the importance of safety. Next, you'll explore ethical foraging, a balance of reaping wild rewards while maintaining their future. You'll also learn how to forage legally, for a worry-free experience. The section on tools will arm you with the essentials for an efficient and sustainable experience. And finally, the chapter offers guidance on harvesting and proper storage.

Safe Foraging

Like any expedition, foraging brings its own thrills and risks. There's a world of edible wonders waiting out there, but also a few risks to be aware of. However, with the right information, some practice, and a mindful approach, you can confidently navigate through the greenscape.

Contrary to what some might think, only a few wild plants in North America are seriously poisonous to adults. Identifying and eliminating these few dangerous ones unveils a world of edible options. When it comes to mushrooms, one principle stands above all: **be absolutely sure before you eat.** Now, let's dive into some safety tips to help you confidently embark on your wild food journey.

The Art of Starting Simple

As a novice, starting with easily identifiable and common edible plants and mushrooms is best. Expand your knowledge and confidence gradually. When preparing wild foods, remember that many need to be cooked. This step is important for neutralizing potential toxins and making them easier to digest.

Slow and Steady Wins the Race

Trying out a new plant or mushroom? Go slow. Start with a small amount and watch out for any adverse reactions. Even within edible species, individual tolerances can vary. The Universal Edibility Test, detailed on the subsequent page, could be your helpful ally when other resources are unavailable. Always introduce new foraged foods gradually into your diet. Even good things can be harmful when consumed in excess.

Know the "Bad Guys"

Start with familiarizing yourself with the local "bad guys," the poisonous species in your area. Learn their unique traits, habitats, and structures. Keep in mind that nature can be tricky, with different plants looking very similar but having completely different effects when eaten. Always double-check to be sure. This book includes photos of poisonous plants that look like edible ones, helping beginners avoid harmful ones.

Trust Your Senses

Stay away from anything with a strong, off-putting smell. Potentially harmful species often use unpleasant odors as warnings; even some edible plants with potent smells might not make for a tasty meal. Trust your instincts.

Pick Your Spot

Opt for places with minimal pollution while choosing foraging locations. Steer clear from contamination hotspots like factories or landfills. And remember, just because animals can eat certain plants doesn't mean we can; humans and animals have different digestive systems. What's edible for them might not be the same for us.

Handle with Care

Be careful when handling your foraged finds. Some plants or mushrooms can cause skin irritation. You can avoid any nasty surprises by wearing gloves, washing your hands, and steering clear of sensitive areas.

Alertness is Your Ally

Learn the signs of poisoning. In the unfortunate case, you consume something harmful, and this knowledge will allow you to act quickly and get medical help. Remember, some toxins show effects right away, while others take time. If you suspect you've been poisoned, don't hesitate to contact a healthcare professional or a poison control center immediately.

The Universal Edibility Test

The Universal Edibility Test (UET) serves as a last resort in determining the safety of unknown plant for consumption. It's **not applicable to mushrooms**, as some poisonous varieties may not cause noticeable symptoms until hours or even days after ingestion. Furthermore, certain plant toxins might evade the UET's detection. Hence, use this method with extreme caution and only when no other reliable information is available. To perform the UET, follow these steps:

1. Observe: Check for signs of disease, insects, or fungus. Skip if it looks unhealthy.

2. Smell: Crush a piece and smell it. An unpleasant odor is a red flag.

3. Separate: Test each part (leaves, stems, roots, flowers, seeds) independently - some may be safe while others are not.

4. Skin Test: Rub a part on your inner wrist. Discard if there's any irritation within 15 minutes.

5. Prepare: Clean and cook if possible to neutralize potential toxins.

6. Taste: Hold a tiny amount of the cooked or raw plant part on your tongue for 15 minutes without swallowing. Discard the plant and rinse your mouth if it causes discomfort.

7. Swallow: If the taste test is clear, swallow a small piece, then avoid all other food or drink for 8 hours, monitoring for signs of illness.

8. Gradual Consumption: If no adverse effects occur after 8 hours, you can slowly eat a bit more, continuing to monitor your body. If still no negative reactions, it's likely safe to eat.

Bear in mind that the UET isn't foolproof. It's far safer to rely on accurate identification and expert knowledge when foraging. Use this test only in emergencies when no other information is accessible.

Ethical Foraging

Ethical foraging goes beyond the mere collection of wild resources, extending into preserving the ecosystems and ensuring their longevity for the future. This practice of mindful harvesting is grounded in respect, consideration, and a vision for a sustainable future. Are you prepared to take on this role? Here's how to begin:

Knowledge is Power

Just like every journey begins with a step, every foraging expedition starts with education. It's about knowing your plants, their ecological role, and the potential impact of harvesting them. Such knowledge will guide your choices on what, when, and how much to gather. Plus, make sure you know about any endangered species in your local area. After all, an informed forager is a responsible one.

Think Long-Term

The saying "take what you need, leave the rest" is the key to foraging that helps the environment. Think about the impact of what you're doing, not just for the land, but for the animals and other people who might want to forage too. Try not to take too much and always leave endangered or rare species alone.

Leave No Trace

Treat the outdoors just like you would your own backyard – with lots of care and respect. Try not to damage plants or disturb where animals live. Leave the place just as you found it. Let's make sure the wild stays wild for generations to come.

Adhering to these principles will help you forge a responsible relationship with the environment, allowing you to enjoy the benefits of foraging while preserving the natural world.

Harvesting Various Parts Responsibly

1. Roots and Underground Stems: Approach with caution. These are the plant's life support; taking them could kill it. Gather sparingly from a small portion of the local plant population.

2. Leaves and Branches: Be gentle when harvesting leaves and branches, taking no more than a quarter from a single plant. This way, the plant lives on, regenerating for future harvests.

3. Flowers, Fruits, and Seeds: With flowers and buds, take just a handful from each plant and only what you need. When it comes to fruits and seeds, leave plenty for the wild animals - they rely on them, too!

4. Mushrooms: Picking mushrooms needs a gentle touch. These fungal fruits are connected to a vast underground network, the mycelium, which must not be damaged. Use a knife to cut mushrooms at the base and gather just a fraction of what's there.

Legal Foraging

Legal Foraging in the U.S.

Navigating the legal aspects of foraging is as intricate as foraging itself. In a land as diverse as the USA, rules and regulations regarding foraging vary extensively across federal, state, and local levels, and may evolve over time.

Public Lands

Public lands are managed at various levels—federal, state, and local—and each comes with its unique set of regulations. Federal public lands include areas like national parks and forests, which are managed by agencies such as the Bureau of Land Management, the National Park Service, and the U.S. Forest Service. Each agency has specific rules, and you can find these on their respective websites.

For national parks specifically, you can refer to the "**Superintendent's Compendium**" on the National Park Service website (https://www.nps.gov). Remember, state and local public lands have their own sets of rules too, so always make sure to research beforehand.

Private Lands

Foraging on private lands demands permission from the landowner. Never assume that unoccupied land is free for foraging—owners can set their own rules.

State Laws

Additionally, state laws might regulate foraging of specific plants or mushroom. An example is Pennsylvania, where ginseng collection on state lands is barred, and harvesting mature plants during harvest season is permitted on private lands. Always review your state's foraging regulations to make sure you're foraging responsibly.

Legal Foraging in Canada

In Canada, foraging laws and regulations vary by province and territory, and they're often intertwined with property rights, conservation efforts, and Indigenous rights. Public lands like national parks, provincial parks, and Crown lands each have their own sets of rules. Generally, foraging is not allowed in national parks, but may be permissible on Crown lands, subject to provincial guidelines. Private lands require owner's permission for any kind of foraging. Laws may also govern specific species; for example, harvesting wild ginseng is strictly regulated in some provinces.

Principles

As you step into the wilderness, keep these guidelines in mind:

Request Permission: Always seek permission before foraging on private land or protected areas. In certain cases, you might need a permit or other authorization.

Respect Boundaries: Respect landowners' rights, avoid damaging private property and be aware of boundaries.

Know Your Laws: Familiarize yourself with all the federal, state, or local rules applicable to the area where you plan to forage, including regulations related to specific plants or mushrooms.

By following these principles, you can ensure that your foraging activities align with legal requirements and are environmentally friendly. For a deeper dive into your area's specific laws and regulations, connect with local authorities or join foraging groups for advice and shared wisdom. After all, foraging is as much about community as it is about personal discovery.

Foraging Tools

Starting a successful foraging trip requires knowledge, skill, and the right tools. These ensure efficiency and productivity. For your foraging adventure, let's examine some essential cutting and digging tools, containers, and other must-haves.

Cutting and Digging Tools

A high-quality foldable knife is key to cutting stems, leaves, and mushrooms without damaging the plant. Pruning shears are perfect for thicker branches, stems, and roots, while a trowel or hand shovel is ideal for unearthing roots, tubers, or bulbs. You might also consider a sturdy digging stick for challenging terrain and a pair of sharp scissors for more delicate plants.

Containers

A lightweight basket, preferably made from natural materials like willow or bamboo, is great for most wild edibles. Consider reusable cloth or mesh bags for lighter items like leaves, flowers, or seeds. Wet or delicate things like berries fare well in lidded plastic containers. A spacious, comfortable backpack is a must for all your gear.

Other Essential Items

Protective gloves shield your hands from thorns and potentially harmful plants. A comprehensive field guide aids in identifying local edible plants and mushrooms. A small hand magnifying glass lets you examine features closely, and a notebook and pen help record your findings and experiences. Navigation aids such as a compass or GPS device ensure you don't lose your way. Lastly, pack a hat and sunscreen to guard against the sun.

Armed with these tools and adhering to basic foraging principles, you'll be ready for a safe, enjoyable, and rewarding journey into the wild.

Harvesting

The optimal time for harvesting different parts of wild plants varies. Leaves are best harvested when young and tender, usually in spring or early summer. Stems can be collected during the plant's active growth period, typically in spring or summer. Flowers should be picked just before or at peak bloom, while fruits are ideal when fully ripe, often in late summer or early fall. Seeds should be gathered when mature and dry, usually in late summer or fall. Roots are best harvested in late fall or early spring when plants store the most nutrients.

The best time to harvest wild mushrooms is during their fruiting period, which depends on the species and local climate. Generally, mushrooms are most abundant in the rainy season or cool, damp conditions. Some species fruit in the spring, while others appear in the summer or fall.

Preserving

Once you have gathered an array of wild plants and mushrooms, storing them properly is essential to preserve their freshness, flavor, and nutritional value. Here, we explore ways to clean, store, and preserve your foraged edibles.

Cleaning and Prepping

Before storing your harvest, gently clean them to remove dirt or debris. For plants, shake them lightly or use a soft brush to remove any soil, and then rinse them in cold water. Use a damp cloth or brush to cleanse the caps and stems of mushrooms. Avoid soaking mushrooms in water, as this can cause them to become soggy.

Storage Containers

Use airtight plastic containers or reusable silicone bags for leafy greens and herbs. For mushrooms, opt for paper bags, wax paper, or breathable containers, which allow moisture to escape and prevent the mushrooms from becoming slimy.

Refrigeration

Refrigerate your wild edibles to extend their shelf life. Store leafy greens and herbs in the crisper drawer, wrapped in a slightly damp paper towel or cloth to maintain humidity. Keep mushrooms in their designated containers in the fridge's main compartment, away from strong-smelling foods.

Drying

Drying is a popular method for preserving foods, especially those with a short shelf life. Spread the plants or mushrooms in a single layer on a clean, dry surface and allow them to air dry for several days. Alternatively, you can also use a food dehydrator to speed up the process. Once completely dry, store them in glass jars or airtight containers, and keep them in a cool, dark place.

Freezing

Blanch leafy greens and herbs in boiling water for a few seconds, then immediately transfer them to ice water to stop cooking. Drain and gently pat them dry before placing them in airtight containers or freezer bags. For mushrooms, sauté them in a bit of oil or butter before freezing, which will help maintain their texture and flavor.

Canning and Pickling

Canning involves heating and sealing the harvest in glass jars, while pickling involves submerging wild plants in a vinegar solution to extend its shelf life. Both methods require proper sterilization and sealing techniques to ensure safe preservation.

Storage Tips

Label your containers with the name and date of harvest. Regularly check for any signs of spoilage, like mold or strange smells. Practice rotating your stock to ensure older items are used first.

By following these guidelines, you can make the most of your foraging adventures, enjoying the flavors and benefits of wild plants and mushrooms even after the foraging season is over.

FORAGER'S TOOLKIT

" *In every walk with nature, one
receives far more than he seeks.* "

John Muir

Welcome to the "Forager's Tool-kit"—a guide that equips you with essential knowledge, secrets, and resources to confidently embark on your foraging journey. You'll start by decoding plant and mushroom taxonomy, laying a firm foundation for identifying wild edibles. Next, you'll explore insider tips and a practical 5-step guide to eliminate guesswork and increase accuracy in plant identification. Finally, you'll employ the Forager's Calendar and Regional Index—invaluable tools that direct your seasonal harvesting and local foraging activities.

Plant & Mushroom Anatomy
Understanding Plant Anatomy

Flowers have four main parts: petals, sepals, pistil, and stamen. Petals are often colorful and fragrant, luring pollinators. Sepals are smaller, green structures that shield the flower bud. The pistil is the flower's female reproductive organ, comprising the stigma, style, and ovary. The stamen, or the male counterpart, consists of the pollen-carrying anther and the filament.

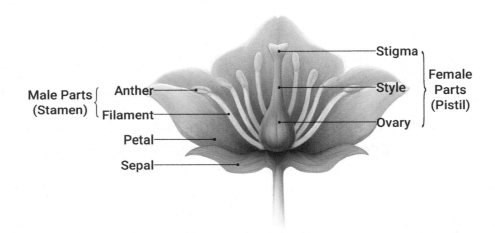

Botanical Names

Safe foraging requires understanding scientific or botanical names. Although common names like velvet bean or death cap are easily recognized, they can lead to confusion as they vary by region and might refer to different species. To solve this issue, 18th-century botanist Carl Linnaeus introduced binomial nomenclature, assigning each organism a unique two-word scientific name. For instance, the dandelion has the botanical name: *Taraxacum officinale*.

Key points on botanical names:

1. Botanical names are Latin and italicized.

2. Composed of two parts, the genus (capitalized) and the species (lowercase). For example, wild onion is *Allium stellatum*, with *Allium* as genus (garlic) and *stellatum* indicating the species with star-like flowers.

3. The genus can be abbreviated (e.g., *A. stellatum*). "spp." refers to multiple species within a single genus. Abbreviations like "sp.", "ssp.", and "var." provide additional classification details.

Leaves consist of the blade, petiole, and stipules. The blade is the photosynthesizing part, often segmented into leaflets. The petiole, a slender stalk, connects the blade to the stem. Stipules are small, leaf-like structures found at the base of the leaf.

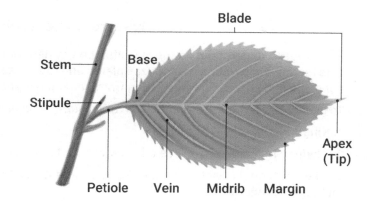

Fruit has the skin, pulp, seeds, core, and stem. The skin, or peel, is the outer layer of the fruit. The pulp, or flesh, is the juicy, sweet portion that contains seeds. Some fruits feature a core, a hard structure housing the seeds. The stem supports the fruit.

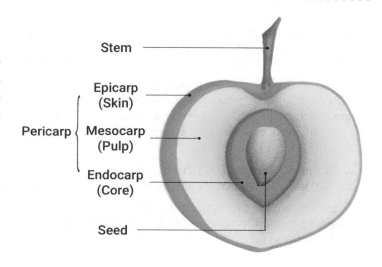

Mushroom Anatomy

Mushrooms, being fungi, differ from plants. The cap, gills, stipe (stem), mycelium, and spores are key parts. The cap shelters the spores and gills. The gills, located beneath the cap, produce and release spores. The stipe elevates the cap. The mycelium is an underground hyphae network absorbing nutrients, while spores are reproductive cells for new mushroom colonies.

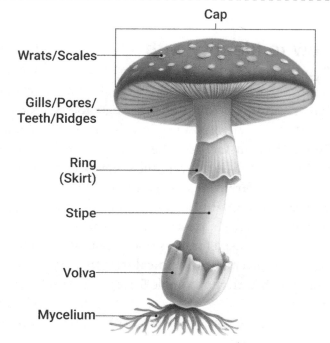

Nature's Hierarchy

For foragers, understanding the classification system of plants and mushrooms is essential. This hierarchical system categorizes plants and mushrooms based on their evolutionary relationships and shared features, going from general (kingdom) to specific (species).

To illustrate, consider the dandelion (*Taraxacum officinale*):

1. **Kingdom**: Plantae - it's a plant.

2. **Phylum**: Magnoliophyta - it's a flowering plant or angiosperm.

3. **Class**: Magnoliopsida - it's a dicot, meaning it has two seed leaves and flower parts in multiples of four or five.

4. **Order**: Asterales - it's part of a diverse group known for their composite flowers and simple leaves.

5. **Family**: Asteraceae (daisy family) - the family of plants with hundreds of individual florets in flower heads.

6. **Genus**: *Taraxacum* - it produces seeds without pollination, has yellow to orange flowers that open during the day and close at night, and exudes white latex when broken.

7. **Species**: *Taraxacum officinale* - the unique name for this specific type of plant.

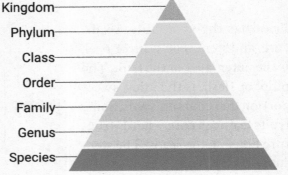

By understanding this system, you're better prepared to identify, understand, and appreciate the plants and mushrooms you encounter while foraging.

How to Identify with Certainty?

Plants and mushrooms change their looks based on their growing environment. Depending on factors like sunlight, soil quality, and moisture levels, the same species can look different in size, color, and other features. Recognizing a plant or mushroom, no matter where it's growing, is the real challenge. Experienced foragers know that looking closely at a plant's botanical structures is more reliable. Here's a simple 5-step guide to help you.

Step 1: Know Your Environment

Start by getting to know your foraging area, whether it's local woodlands, lakesides, or open fields. This understanding aids in identifying species. Take photos and notes about the habitat, location, growth stage, and season, as these factors influence plant and mushroom appearances. For mushrooms, observe the substrate (soil, wood, or other organic material), surrounding vegetation, and conditions like moisture and shade. These details help pinpoint specific species.

Step 2: Inspect Reliable Traits

Next, focus on the botanical attributes of the plant or mushroom. While size and color can vary due to environmental influences, certain traits remain consistent within a species or family, which can significantly enhance the accuracy of your identification process. These key traits include:

LEAVES: Are they simple or compound? What about their edges - are they smooth, toothed, or lobed? Also, consider the leaf veins and their branching patterns.

STEMS: Note whether the stem is woody, herbaceous, or succulent. Further, observe whether it is hollow, solid, or filled with milky sap.

FLOWERS: Count the number of petals, sepals, and reproductive structures (stamens and pistils). Assess the symmetry of the flower, its fragrance, and whether it grows alone or in clusters. These characteristics often differ widely between plant families and can be a key to the plant's identity.

FRUITS AND SEEDS: How is the fruit attached to the plant? Is it fleshy or dry? Observe the seed's size, shape, color, and specialized structures like wings or hooks for seed dispersal.

ROOTS: Though not always applicable for foragers, observing the root can provide valuable insights if feasible. Is it fibrous, or does it have a taproot? Note the size, color, and texture of the roots.

In the case of mushrooms, you would need to focus on these:

CAP: Observe its shape, color, and texture. Does the cap change color when bruised or scratched? Is it slimy, dry, or scaly? What is the shape of the cap - convex, flat, conical, or umbonate?

GILLS/PORES/TEETH/RIDGES: Look at the structures on the underside of the cap. Note their color, the spacing between them, and attachment to the stipe (if present). Do they bruise or stain when touched?

STIPE (STEM): Look for a ring (also known as an annulus) or a volva at the base of the stipe. These structures, when present, can provide important clues about the mushroom's identity.

SPORE PRINT: A spore print is made by placing the mushroom cap on paper and allowing the spores to drop. The resulting pattern and color can help confirm a mushroom's identity. See "Making a Spore Print" on page 22.

Step 3: Use Your Other Senses

Don't just look at the plant or mushroom; use your other senses too. Many plants have a unique smell or taste that can help you tell them apart. But remember, only taste a plant if you're sure it's not poisonous. The scent of a mushroom can be a valuable clue in identifying it. Try to familiarize yourself with the unique smells of various mushroom species.

Step 4: Beware of Poisonous Look-alikes

Safety comes first. Ensure you know about the common poisonous plants and mushrooms in your area. Many guides and online resources can help you tell the difference between safe and harmful species. If you're unsure, ask someone who knows, like an experienced forager or a local expert. Remember, **if you can't confidently identify a plant or mushroom, it's better to avoid touching or eating it.**

Step 5: Double-Check and Learn

Double-check your findings with other sources. Also, keep watching the plant or mushroom over time and note how it changes. This will help you get familiar with it and improve your identification skills.

In short, identifying wild plants and mushrooms can be challenging, but you can improve over time with some patience and practice. The secret to successful foraging is observing closely, examining carefully, and always learning more.

Making a Spore Print

A spore print is a critical tool for mushroom identification, revealing the unique spore pattern and color.

1. To make one, you need a mature mushroom, black and white paper, a bowl or glass, and a knife.

2. Cut off the mushroom stem to expose the cap's underside.

3. Lay the black paper down with the white paper on top for contrast. Center the cap on the paper, underside down.

4. Cover it with a bowl or glass, and leave it undisturbed for several hours or overnight.

5. Upon lifting the bowl and cap, you'll find the spore print on the paper.

This color and pattern will aid your mushroom identification.

Pro Tips: Finding Family Traits

A key strategy adopted by experienced foragers is identifying plant families before moving to individual species. This approach is beneficial for a few reasons:

1. Efficiency: Identifying plant families allows for quick elimination of unrelated species that might only bear a superficial resemblance, making the process more efficient.

2. Safety: Certain plant families are known for a high proportion of edible species. Familiarity with these families can minimize the risk of ingesting poisonous plants. For instance, the Brassicaceae (mustard) family consists of numerous edible plants, known to be safe for consumption.

3. Similar Traits and Uses: Plants within a family often share features and uses. Brassicaceae plants, for example, are rich in vita-

mins, minerals, and phytonutrients.

On the contrary, mushrooms are a different case. Unlike plants, identifying mushrooms by families isn't as reliable. The reason is that mushrooms can be highly variable, and their edibility can change based on age, growing conditions, and individual sensitivities. Therefore, it's critical to accurately identify each mushroom and refer to trustworthy sources, ensuring a safe mushroom foraging experience.

Family Traits Examples

Below are some common plant families with their distinct traits:

1. Asteraceae (the aster family, plant no. 19-29 in the book): The most defining feature of this family is their inflorescence or flower structure. What often appears as a single flower is actually a composite of many smaller flowers, or florets. These are usually arranged in a tight cluster, that is typically surrounded by petal-like structures called ray florets (that form the "petals" of the flower head) and disk florets that form the center.

2. Brassicaceae (the mustard family, plant no. 30-36 in the book): Brassicaceae flowers usually have four free sepals and four clawed free petals, arranged diagonally. The flowers tend to be bisexual and are often in the shape of a cross. The flowers are usually organized in a raceme, which is an unbranched, indeterminate type of inflorescence.

3. Lamiaceae (the mint family, plant no. 55-58 in the book): Plants in this family generally have simple, opposite leaves that are often aromatic due to the presence of essential oils. The stems are typically square-shaped or four-sided, which is a distinct characteristic of the mint family. The flowers are often brightly colored, bilaterally symmetrical, and usually are arranged in clusters.

Forager's Calendar

The calendar paints a broad picture of when edible parts of plants and mushrooms are typically abundant across North America. It's a starting point, not a strict schedule. Regional differences can alter this timeline. Furthermore, many plants offer the tastiest harvest when young and fresh. So, keep a keen eye on each plant's growth stages to tailor your timeline to the ideal harvesting time.

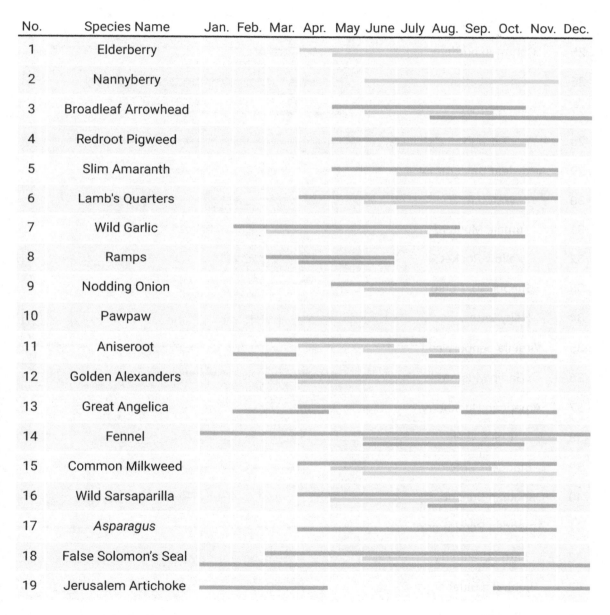

No.	Species Name	Jan.	Feb.	Mar.	Apr.	May	June	July	Aug.	Sep.	Oct.	Nov.	Dec.
1	Elderberry												
2	Nannyberry												
3	Broadleaf Arrowhead												
4	Redroot Pigweed												
5	Slim Amaranth												
6	Lamb's Quarters												
7	Wild Garlic												
8	Ramps												
9	Nodding Onion												
10	Pawpaw												
11	Aniseroot												
12	Golden Alexanders												
13	Great Angelica												
14	Fennel												
15	Common Milkweed												
16	Wild Sarsaparilla												
17	*Asparagus*												
18	False Solomon's Seal												
19	Jerusalem Artichoke												

Important! Listing in the calendar doesn't guarantee safety or edibility. Ensure you read the full descriptions of each plant and mushroom in this book for optimal harvest and consumption.

Stems & leaves: ▬▬▬ Fruits & seeds & nuts: ▬▬▬ Mushroom fruiting body: ▬▬▬
Flowers: ▬▬▬ Underground parts: ▬▬▬

No.	Species Name	Jan.	Feb.	Mar.	Apr.	May	June	July	Aug.	Sep.	Oct.	Nov.	Dec.
20	Canada lettuce												
21	Sow Thistle												
22	Dandelion												
23	Purple Salsify												
24	Chicory												
25	Common burdock												
26	Prickly Lettuce												
27	Yarrow												
28	Tarragon												
29	Arrowleaf Balsamroot												
30	Watercress												
31	Tumble Mustard												
32	Yellow Rocket												
33	Shepherd's Purse												
34	Hairy Bittercress												
35	Virginia pepperweed												
36	Garlic Mustard												
37	American Hackberry												
38	Chickweed												
39	Bladder Campion												
40	Canadian Bunchberry												
41	American Persimmon												
42	Large Cranberry												
43	Highbush Blueberry												
44	Bog Blueberry												
45	Wintergreen												
46	Groundnut												

No.	Species Name	Jan.	Feb.	Mar.	Apr.	May	June	July	Aug.	Sep.	Oct.	Nov.	Dec.
47	Alfalfa				▬	▬	▬	▬	▬	▬	▬		
48	Yellow Sweet Clover					▬	▬	▬	▬	▬	▬		
49	White Clover			▬	▬	▬	▬	▬	▬	▬			
50	Hog-peanut	▬	▬								▬	▬	▬
51	American Beech	▬	▬	▬	▬	▬	▬	▬	▬	▬	▬	▬	▬
52	White Oak			▬	▬	▬	▬	▬	▬	▬	▬		
53	Black Walnut				▬	▬	▬	▬	▬	▬	▬		
54	Shagbark Hickory				▬	▬	▬	▬	▬	▬	▬		
55	Creeping Charlie			▬	▬	▬	▬	▬	▬	▬	▬	▬	
56	Bee Balm				▬	▬	▬	▬	▬	▬			
57	Self-heal			▬	▬	▬	▬	▬	▬	▬	▬	▬	
58	Anise Hyssop					▬	▬	▬	▬	▬	▬	▬	
59	Sassafras			▬	▬	▬	▬	▬	▬	▬	▬		
60	Paper Mulberry			▬	▬	▬	▬	▬	▬	▬	▬	▬	▬
61	Evening Primrose			▬	▬	▬	▬	▬	▬	▬	▬	▬	
62	Fireweed					▬	▬	▬	▬	▬	▬	▬	
63	Plantain			▬	▬	▬	▬	▬	▬	▬	▬		
64	American Brooklime				▬	▬	▬	▬	▬	▬	▬		
65	Common Reed	▬	▬	▬	▬	▬	▬	▬		▬	▬	▬	▬
66	Lady's thumb				▬	▬	▬	▬	▬	▬	▬	▬	
67	Knotweed					▬	▬	▬	▬	▬	▬	▬	
68	Wild Strawberry				▬	▬	▬	▬	▬	▬	▬		
69	American Plum					▬	▬	▬	▬	▬	▬	▬	▬
70	Red Raspberry			▬	▬	▬	▬	▬	▬	▬	▬		
71	Allegheny Blackberry			▬	▬	▬	▬	▬	▬	▬	▬		
72	Woods' Rose			▬	▬	▬	▬	▬	▬	▬	▬		
73	Common Hawthorn			▬	▬	▬	▬	▬	▬	▬	▬	▬	

No.	Species Name	Jan.	Feb.	Mar.	Apr.	May	June	July	Aug.	Sep.	Oct.	Nov.	Dec.
74	Saskatoon Berry					●	●	●	●	●	●		
75	Sweet Woodruff			●	●	●	●	●	●	●	●	●	
76	Cattail	●	●	●	●	●	●	●	●	●	●	●	●
77	Stinging Nettle			●	●	●	●	●	●	●	●	●	
78	Common Blue Violet		●	●	●	●	●	●					
79	Riverbank Grape				●	●	●	●	●	●	●	●	
80	Orange Daylily	●	●	●	●	●	●	●	●	●		●	●
81	Meadow Mushroom				●	●	●	●	●	●	●	●	●
82	Horse Mushroom				●	●	●	●	●	●	●	●	●
83	The Prince				●	●	●	●	●	●	●	●	●
84	Shaggy Ink Cap								●	●	●	●	●
85	King Bolete	●						●	●	●	●	●	●
86	Birch Bolete							●	●	●	●	●	●
87	Beefsteak Mushroom							●	●	●	●	●	●
88	Chicken of the Woods				●	●	●	●	●	●	●	●	●
89	Lion's Mane	●	●	●					●	●	●	●	●
90	The Deceiver	●	●	●	●	●	●	●	●	●	●	●	●
91	Lobster Mushroom							●	●	●	●	●	●
92	Hen of the Woods								●	●	●	●	●
93	Black Morel				●	●	●						
94	Honey Fungus	●							●	●	●	●	●
95	Oyster Mushroom	●	●	●	●	●	●	●	●	●	●	●	●
96	Dryad's Saddle			●	●	●	●	●	●	●	●	●	●
97	Saffron Milk Cap	●	●	●				●	●	●	●	●	●
98	Charcoal Burner							●	●	●	●	●	●
99	Weeping Bolete					●	●	●	●	●	●	●	●
100	Aniseed Toadstool							●	●	●	●	●	●

Regional Index

This section provides a concise guide to foraging across the U.S. and Canada. Each state, province, and territory is listed alphabetically, paired with reference numbers for the plant and mushroom species found there as covered in this book. Use this index to quickly navigate and identify the botanical treasures specific to your region of interest.

U.S. Regional Index

States and District	Plant & Mushroom Reference No.
Alabama	1-12, 15, 17-22, 24-27, 30, 32-35, 37-38, 41, 43, 45-57, 59-61, 63, 65-67, 69, 71, 76-78, 80-82, 84-97, 99
Alaska	4, 6, 18, 21-22, 27-28, 30-31, 33, 35-36, 38-40, 44, 47-49, 55, 57, 62-64, 66-67, 70, 72-74, 76-77, 81-86, 88-91, 93-100
Arizona	1, 3-6, 9, 14, 17-18, 21-31, 33-35, 38, 47-49, 56-57, 62-70, 72, 76-77, 81-85, 87-91, 93-95, 97, 99-100
Arkansas	1, 3-7, 9-12, 15, 17-27, 30-39, 41, 43, 46-57, 59-61, 63-67, 69-71, 73, 76, 78-80, 82, 84, 86-95, 97, 100
California	1, 3-6, 14, 17-35, 38-39, 41-42, 44, 47-49, 55, 57, 61-66, 68, 70-74, 76-77, 81-91, 93-100
Colorado	1-6, 9, 11, 16-33, 35-40, 46-49, 53, 55-58, 62-70, 72, 74-77, 79-91, 93-100
Connecticut	1-8, 10-28, 30-43, 45-71, 73, 76-82, 84-92, 94-100
Delaware	1, 3-8, 10-27, 30-39, 41-43, 45-71, 73, 75-78, 80-82, 84-92, 94-100
District of Columbia	1, 3-12, 15-27, 30-38, 41, 43, 45-57, 59-63, 65-67, 69, 71, 73, 76-100
Florida	1, 3-7, 10, 12, 14, 17-22, 24, 26-27, 30-35, 37-38, 41, 43, 46-53, 55, 57, 59-61, 63, 65-67, 69, 76-78, 80-92, 94-95, 97-99
Georgia	1-12, 14-27, 30-39, 41, 43, 45-57, 59-61, 63, 65-67, 69, 71, 75-78, 80-82, 84-92, 94-99
Hawaii	1, 3-6, 14, 21-23, 26-27, 31, 33-35, 38, 47-49, 57, 60, 63, 65, 67-68, 76, 81-82, 84, 88, 94-95, 99
Idaho	3-6, 9, 16-33, 35-36, 38-40, 44, 47-49, 55-57, 62-68, 70, 72, 74, 76-77, 80-82, 84-85, 88, 90-91, 93-97, 99-100
Illinois	1-28, 30-43, 45-71, 73, 76-82, 84-100
Indiana	1-13, 15-27, 30-43, 45-57, 59-71, 76-100

States and District	Plant & Mushroom Reference No.
Iowa	1-28, 30-33, 35-41, 46-50, 52-59, 61-72, 74, 76-82, 84-97, 99-100
Kansas	1, 3-7, 10-12, 14-15, 17-28, 30-33, 35-39, 41, 46-50, 52-57, 59-61, 63-67, 69, 71-72, 76-82, 84-96, 98-100
Kentucky	1-27, 30-39, 41, 43, 45-61, 63-69, 71, 73, 76-81, 84, 86-92, 94-97, 99-100
Louisiana	1, 3-7, 10, 12, 14-15, 17-22, 24-27, 30-31, 33-35, 38, 41, 43, 46-57, 59-61, 63, 65-67, 69, 76-81, 84-92, 94-95, 98-99
Maine	1-8, 11-27, 30-33, 35-36, 38-40, 42-57, 59, 61-71, 73, 76-82, 84-92, 94-100
Maryland	1-27, 30-43, 45-57, 59-71, 75-82, 84-100
Massachusetts	1-8, 11-28, 30-43, 45-57, 59-71, 73, 75-82, 84-92, 94-100
Michigan	1-27, 30-40, 42-59, 61-71, 73, 75-82, 84-100
Minnesota	1-9, 11-13, 15-22, 24-28, 30-33, 35-40, 42, 44-58, 61-72, 74-100
Mississippi	1, 3-7, 9-12, 14-15, 17-22, 24-27, 30-31, 33-35, 37-38, 41, 43, 46-57, 59-61, 63, 65-67, 69, 76-78, 80-81, 84-95
Missouri	1-12, 14-28, 30-39, 41, 46-57, 59-61, 63-71, 76-82, 84-85, 87-92, 94-100
Montana	1-7, 9, 11-12, 15-33, 35, 37-40, 44, 47-50, 55-58, 61-70, 72-74, 76-77, 79-86, 88, 90-91, 93-95, 97, 99-100
Nebraska	1-7, 9-12, 14-28, 30-33, 35-39, 41, 46-50, 52-58, 61-72, 74, 76-82, 84-85, 88, 91-92, 94-97
Nevada	4-6, 14, 17-18, 21-31, 33, 35, 38, 44, 47-49, 56-57, 61-67, 72, 74, 76-77, 81, 84-86, 95, 100
New Hampshire	1-8, 11-13, 15-27, 30-33, 35-40, 42-59, 61-71, 73, 76-82, 84-92, 94-100
New Jersey	1-28, 30-43, 45-71, 73, 75-82, 84-92, 94-100
New Mexico	1, 3-6, 9, 11, 14, 17-18, 20-28, 30-35, 37-40, 47-49, 53, 56-57, 61-70, 72, 74, 76-77, 81-85, 89-97, 99-100
New York	1-28, 30-71, 73, 75-92, 94-100
North Carolina	1, 3-27, 30-39, 41-43, 45-57, 59-71, 75-100

States and District	Plant & Mushroom Reference No.
North Dakota	1-8, 11-12, 15-22, 24-29, 31-33, 35-40, 46-50, 53-58, 61-70, 72, 74, 76-79, 81-82, 84-85, 87-88, 94-95
Ohio	1-27, 30-43, 45-57, 59-71, 73, 75-100
Oklahoma	1, 3-8, 10-12, 15, 17-28, 30-38, 41, 43, 46-57, 59-61, 63-67, 69-72, 76-79, 81-82, 84, 87-92, 94-95, 100
Oregon	3-6, 9, 14-15, 17-36, 38-40, 42, 44, 47-49, 55-57, 61-68, 70, 72-77, 79-91, 93-95, 97-100
Pennsylvania	1-27, 30-43, 45-71, 73, 75-100
Rhode Island	1-8, 11-22, 24-27, 30-33, 35, 37-40, 42-43, 45-57, 59-71, 73, 75-82, 84-92, 94-100
South Carolina	1, 3-7, 9-12, 14-22, 24-27, 30-39, 41, 43, 45-57, 59-61, 63-67, 69, 71, 76-78, 80-81, 84-96, 98-100
South Dakota	1-9, 11-12, 15-33, 35, 37-40, 46-50, 53, 55-58, 61-70, 72, 74, 76-80, 84-85, 88, 91, 94-95, 99
Tennessee	1, 3-27, 30-39, 41-43, 45-57, 59-71, 73, 76-82, 84-100
Texas	1, 3-7, 9-12, 14-15, 17-28, 30-31, 33-35, 37-38, 41, 43, 46-57, 59-61, 63-68, 72, 76-82, 84-85, 87-92, 94-95, 97-98, 100
Utah	3-4, 6, 9, 14, 17-33, 35-39, 41, 44, 47-49, 51, 53, 55-57, 62-70, 72-74, 76-77, 80-85, 88-90, 93-100
Vermont	1-8, 11-13, 15-27, 30-33, 35-40, 42-52, 54-57, 59, 61-71, 73, 76-82, 84-92, 94-100
Virginia	1-12, 14-27, 30-43, 45-57, 59-71, 73, 75-100
Washington	3-6, 9, 14, 16-36, 38-40, 42-44, 47-49, 55-58, 61-70, 72-77, 79-91, 93-100
West Virginia	1-27, 30-43, 45-57, 59-71, 73, 76-100
Wisconsin	1-28, 30-33, 35-40, 42-43, 45-59, 61-73, 76-100
Wyoming	1-4, 6, 9, 11, 16-33, 35, 37-40, 44, 47-50, 55-58, 62-70, 72, 74, 76-77, 79-82, 84-85, 90-91, 94-95, 97, 99

Canada Regional Index

Provinces and Territories	Plant & Mushroom Reference No.
Alberta	3-4, 6, 9, 11, 14-18, 20-33, 38-40, 44, 47-49, 55-58, 61-66, 68, 70, 72, 74, 76-77, 81-86, 88, 90-91, 93, 95, 97-100
British Columbia	3-4, 6, 9, 14-18, 20-36, 38-40, 42-44, 47-49, 55-58, 61-66, 68, 70-77, 81-86, 88, 90-100
Manitoba	1-6, 8, 11-12, 15-28, 30-33, 37-40, 44-45, 47-50, 53, 55-58, 61-66, 68-70, 72, 74, 76-77, 79, 81, 84, 86-95
New Brunswick	1-4, 6-8, 11-13, 15-27, 30-33, 35-36, 38-40, 42-51, 55, 57-58, 61-66, 68, 70-71, 73-74, 76-77, 79-82, 84-86, 88-92, 94-100
Newfoundland and Labrador	3-4, 6, 13, 16-18, 20-22, 24-25, 27, 31-33, 35, 38-40, 42, 44-45, 47-49, 55, 57, 61-68, 70, 76-77, 81-82, 84-86, 88, 90, 97, 99-100
Northwest Territories	4, 6, 16, 18, 21-22, 27, 31, 33, 38, 40, 42, 44, 47-49, 56, 58, 62-68, 70, 72, 74, 76-77, 81, 84, 86, 97
Nova Scotia	1, 3-6, 8, 11-13, 15-27, 30-33, 35-36, 38-40, 42-51, 55, 57, 61-66, 68, 70-71, 73, 76-77, 79-81, 84-86, 88-92, 94-97, 99-100
Nunavut	22, 27, 33, 40, 44, 62, 70, 85
Ontario	1-28, 30-40, 42-59, 61-66, 68-100
Prince Edward Island	1, 3-4, 6, 11, 13, 15-22, 24-27, 31-33, 35, 38-40, 42, 44-49, 51, 55, 57, 61-66, 70-71, 73, 76-77, 80-82, 84-86, 88-92, 94-97, 99-100
Quebec	1-8, 11-27, 30-40, 42-58, 61-100
Saskatchewan	2-4, 6, 9, 11, 15-19, 21-22, 24-28, 30-33, 38-40, 44, 47-49, 55-58, 61-70, 72, 74, 76-78, 81, 84-85, 88, 95
Yukon	6, 16, 20, 22, 27-28, 31, 33, 38-40, 44, 47-49, 57, 62-64, 66-67, 70, 72, 74, 76-77, 81-84, 86, 93-94, 97-98

EDIBLE PLANTS

FLOWER: Small, lemon-scented, creamy-white, and have five petals; arranged in large flat-topped or rounded clusters (cymes) that measure up to 10 inches (25 cm) across.

FRUIT: Clusters of rounded, purplish-black drupes about 0.2 inches (5 mm) in diameter. Each drupe contains 3 to 5 seeds and has a thin skin enveloping a juicy pulp.

EDIBLE USE: Berries have a tart flavor, making them a popular ingredient in pies. They can also be transformed into elderberry wine, a traditional homemade beverage with a unique fruity taste. Elderberry syrup, prepared by simmering the berries with sugar and water, serves as a versatile topping for pancakes, waffles, or ice cream. Flowers are edible, consumed fresh, cooked, or transformed into a light, sweet tea.

MEDICINAL USE: Inner bark, leaves, and flowers exhibit anti-inflammatory, diaphoretic, diuretic, and expectorant properties; aid in treating colds, flu, fever, coughs, bronchitis, sinusitis, and allergies; can be applied externally as a poultice or wash for wounds.

HARVESTING: Fruits should be harvested when ripe and dark purple-black in color. Flowers should be picked when fully open and fragrant in late spring and summer.

CAUTION: Do not eat any part of the plant raw except the flowers. The leaves, stems, roots, seeds, and unripe fruits contain cyanogenic glycosides that can cause poisoning.

1 Elderberry
Sambucus canadensis

IDENTIFICATION FEATURES

BARK: Yellowish-gray to grayish-brown bark with white pith.

LEAF: Compound with 5 to 11 leaflets (usually 7) opposite on the stem. The leaflets are 2 to 6 inches (5-15 cm) long and 0.5 to 2.5 inches (1-6 cm) wide, with sharply serrated margins and pointed tips. The upper surface of the leaflets is dark green and smooth, while the lower surface is lighter green and may be either hairy or hairless at times.

OTHER NAMES: Sheepberry, sweetberry

HEIGHT: 10-18 feet (3-5.5 m) tall as a shrub, up to 30 feet (9 m) as a small tree

HABITATS: Moist areas such as low woods, swamp borders, or near stream banks

EDIBLE PARTS: Berries

2 Nannyberry
Viburnum lentago

IDENTIFICATION FEATURES

BARK: Grayish-brown and can have shallow furrows or ridges, with a somewhat rough appearance and a few fine cracks.

LEAF: The leaves are opposite, simple, and measure 2-4 inches (5-10 cm) in length and 1-2 inches (2.5-5 cm) in width. They have an ovate shape with a finely serrated margin and glossy dark green color. The leaves have pointed tips and display red and burgundy hues during the fall. The leaf stalks are reddish-brown.

FLOWER: Creamy white, 5 petals and long stamens, non-fragrant, borne in flat-topped cymes that are 2-5 inches (5-13 cm) across.

FRUIT: Blue-black, berry-like drupes, 1/3 inch (8.5 mm) long, containing a single seed; ripen in autumn and persist into winter; sweet taste with slight bitterness or sourness; rich in vitamin C and antioxidants.

EDIBLE USE: Freshly harvested berries can be enjoyed raw or added to fruit salads. They are highly favored for making jams, jellies, and preserves. They can also be baked into pies or puddings, where their subtle sweetness complements fruits like apples or pears. Drying the berries allows for long-term storage, providing a sweet treat or cooking ingredient throughout winter.

MEDICINAL USE: Leaves can be brewed into a tea with astringent, diuretic, and antispas-modic effects; bark and roots are used to treat headaches, toothaches, rheumatism, cramps, skin infections, and nervous disorders.

HARVESTING: Best time to pick the fruits is when they are soft to the touch and fully ripe; gently pull them from the stems or cut using pruning shears; store in a cool and dry place for several weeks or frozen for longer preservation.

CAUTION: Fruits contain a small amount of cyanide that can cause nausea or vomiting if eaten in large quantities; cyanide is mostly concentrated in the seeds, so it is advisable to remove them before eating; it may cause allergic reactions in some people who are sensitive to elderberries or honeysuckles.

General Information

OTHER NAMES: Duck-potato, katniss, wapato

HEIGHT: 1-4 feet (0.3-1.2 m) tall when not submerged

HABITATS: Marshes, swamps, lakes, rivers, streams, wetland margins

EDIBLE PARTS: Tubers, young leaves, shoots, buds

FRUIT: Brown achenes (dry fruits) that are 0.1-0.16 inch (2.5-4 mm) long. The achenes are clustered together in spherical heads.

TUBER: Starchy tubers that are rounded, fleshy, and have brown or black outer skin.

EDIBLE USE: The tubers are highly versatile in the kitchen. They can be boiled or baked, similar to potatoes, and served as a side dish. They can also be mashed or used in soups or stews. The young shoots and leaves of the plant are also edible. Boiling these parts yields a tasty vegetable dish, which can be seasoned and served as a standalone side or incorporated into a wider range of recipes, such as stir-fries or pasta dishes. The unopened flower buds can be pickled.

MEDICINAL USE: Tubers are used to treat indigestion, diarrhea, dysentery, and stomach ulcers, and leaves are used to treat wounds, burns, skin infections, and insect bites.

HARVESTING: Tubers can be harvested from late summer to early winter by digging them up from the mud or by pulling them up by their stalks; the leaves and shoots can be picked in spring and summer, and the flowers can be picked in summer and early fall.

CAUTION: The plant may contain oxalates, which can cause kidney stones or interfere with calcium absorption if consumed in large amounts; people with kidney problems or gout should avoid eating this plant.

3 Broadleaf Arrowhead
Sagittaria latifolia

IDENTIFICATION FEATURES

STEM: Erect or floating stems emerging from the water or mud.

LEAF: Basal leaves of the plant can vary in shape depending on water depth and the age of the plant. They can be arrowhead-shaped with backward-facing lobes or points, heart-shaped, spear-shaped, or narrow and elongated. They have smooth edges, no hairs, and prominent veins that radiate from the base to the tip.

FLOWER: White flowers with yellow centers, arranged in whorls of three on long stalks that rise above the water or mud surface. Flowers are saucer-shaped, 0.4-0.8 inch (10-20 mm) long.

4 Redroot Pigweed
Amaranthus retroflexus

IDENTIFICATION FEATURES

STEM: Erect, green to red-streaked, covered with white hairs.

LEAF: Green or reddish-green, nearly 6 inches (15 cm) long on large individuals; higher leaves are lance-shaped, while the lower ones are diamond or oval-shaped, with prominent veins.

FLOWER: Small, greenish, arranged in dense spikes at the top of the stem or in the leaf axils, unisexual, with male and female flowers on the same plant.

FRUIT: Capsules that are round or oval, smooth or wrinkled, brown or black when mature, containing one seed each.

SEED: Small, black, contained within a capsule.

EDIBLE USE: The young leaves and shoots can be cooked in many ways, similar to spinach. They can be sautéed with garlic and oil for a simple dish, steamed and served with a drizzle of olive oil and some sea salt, or added to soups and stews for extra nutrition and texture. The seeds of the plant are small but can be collected in quantity. They can be cooked like a grain, serving as a base for dishes like pilafs or grain salads. Alternatively, they can be ground into flour and used in baking, lending a unique, earthy flavor to breads, muffins, and other baked goods.

MEDICINAL USE: Used in traditional medicine for its purported anti-inflammatory and analgesic properties. It is also believed to aid digestion and has been used to treat diarrhea and dysentery.

HARVESTING: Leaves are best harvested when young and tender, before flowering and seed production. Seeds ripen from July to October.

CAUTION: Leaves contain oxalic acid and may contain nitrates if grown in nitrate-rich soils. It is recommended to discard the water after boiling the leaves and to avoid eating large quantities of leaves. It can cause gastrointestinal irritation and kidney damage if ingested in large amounts.

5 Slim Amaranth
Amaranthus hybridus

General Information

OTHER NAMES: Green amaranth, smooth pigweed, red amaranth

HEIGHT: 1-8 feet (0.3–2.5 m) tall

HABITATS: Railroads, roadsides, riverbanks, meadows, fields, gardens

EDIBLE PARTS: Leaves, seeds

IDENTIFICATION FEATURES

STEM: Thick, often branched. It may have a ribbed texture or a red tinge. Stem surfaces have fine hairs. Cross-section may be round or oval.

LEAF: Shapes vary from spear-like to oval or diamond-like, ranging from 1-7.5 inches (2.5-19 cm) long and 0.6-3 inches (1.5-8 cm) wide. Tips are pointed or blunt, with a wedge-shaped base. Edges are smooth, and undersides may have sparse hair along the edges and veins, which may be pink or red.

FLOWER: Can be yellowish, green, reddish, or purple, located in spikes formed from small clusters at stem ends and leaf axils. Each is protected by a longer bract.

FRUIT: Oval or elongated oval, 0.06-0.1 inches (1.5-2.5 mm) long; lid may be wart-like or rough.

SEED: Black or dark reddish-brown, lens-shaped, and 0.04-0.05 inches (1-1.3 mm).

EDIBLE USE: The young leaves can be eaten raw in salads or cooked for various dishes. Sautéed with oil and garlic, they provide a simple, flavorful side. They can also be added to soups or stews or incorporated into stir-fries, curries, or pasta dishes. The seeds, although small, are plentiful and nutritious. They can be cooked as a grain or popped like popcorn, ground into flour, or cooked as cereal.

MEDICINAL USE: Used to lower blood pressure, reduce inflammation, treat diarrhea, heal wounds, and improve skin conditions.

HARVESTING: It is optimal to collect the leaves while they are still young and tender, typically before the plant reaches a height of two feet. The seeds are ready for collection when they are dry from mid-summer to winter.

CAUTION: Avoid eating large amounts of raw leaves or seeds, as they may contain oxalic acid or saponins. Consult your doctor before using amaranth medicinally.

General Information

OTHER NAMES: White goosefoot, pigweed, fat hen

HEIGHT: Up to 6 feet (1.8 m) tall

HABITATS: Roadsides, gardens, fields, waste areas, and coastal beaches.

EDIBLE PARTS: Young leaves, shoots, seeds, flowers

6 Lamb's Quarter
Chenopodium album

IDENTIFICATION FEATURES

STEM: Erect, branched, green to red or purple striped, often purple at the leaf nodes.

LEAF: Alternate, simple leaves that are goose foot-shaped, or may be triangle, spearhead, thin rectangle, or oval-shaped, with toothed or lobed margins. Upper surface is green or gray-green, while lower surface is covered with a white powdery substance.

FLOWER: Small, greenish, and inconspicuous flowers arranged in dense clusters at the tips of branches or in leaf axils. No petals, with 5 stamens. Wind-pollinated.

SEED: Tiny, black or green, rounded seeds.

EDIBLE USE: Young leaves and shoots can be eaten raw in salads, providing a crunchy texture and a light, pleasant flavor. They can also be sautéed with garlic and oil, steamed, or added to soups or stews. The seeds of the plant can be cooked like a grain, similar to quinoa, or ground into a flour for baking. The young inflorescences of the plant, when still tightly packed and green, can be cooked and eaten like broccoli. They can be steamed, sautéed, or incorporated into dishes like pasta, stir-fries, or grain bowls.

MEDICINAL USE: This plant is utilized for an array of conditions, including gastrointestinal disorders, skin infections, and rheumatism.

HARVESTING: Young leaves are preferred, gathered pre-flowering. Seeds are harvested late summer to fall. After drying and separating from the seed heads, they can be kept in an airtight container for later use.

CAUTION: Contains oxalic acid and possibly high levels of nitrates, particularly if grown in areas with chemical exposure. It may have accumulated high levels of nitrates from fertilizers or manure, which can cause nitrate poisoning if consumed in large amounts.

7 Wild Garlic
Allium canadense

IDENTIFICATION FEATURES

STEM: Stiffly erect flowering stalks, similar in height to the leaves or slightly taller. The stems are round in cross-section, straight, and smooth, emitting a strong, aromatic onion-like smell.

LEAF: 6-12 inches (15-30 cm) long, linear, and flat green leaves. They originate near stem base and resemble grass when young.

FLOWER: Topped by a dome-like cluster of star-shaped flowers that can be pink, purple, or white. The flowers, often 1/2 inch (1.2 cm) in size, may be replaced by bulblets.

FRUIT: Brown capsule, less than 1 inch (2.5 cm) in length and width. It contains several tiny, dark seeds.

BULB: Edible bulb, covered with a dense skin of brown fibers.

ODOR: A strong, onion-like odor is produced when the leaves are crushed.

EDIBLE USE: The bulbs, leaves, and flowers are edible and can serve as onion or garlic substitutes. The bulb can be consumed raw or cooked, with a mild flavor resembling leek or garlic. It can be used as a seasoning or a substitute for onion in salads, soups, stews, and other dishes. The leaves can be used similarly to chives, chopped and sprinkled on top

of dishes. The flowers can be used as a garnish or incorporated into salads.

MEDICINAL USE: The bulb has antibacterial, antifungal, antiseptic, and anti-inflammatory properties, used to treat external wounds and internal ailments like coughs and digestive issues. The leaves and flowers have similar but varying intensities of these properties.

HARVESTING: Flowers can be harvested in the spring and summer. Harvest the bulb with a knife or a trowel, and clean it before storage. Be mindful of potential pesticide exposure.

CAUTION: Consumption can lead to allergic reactions or gastrointestinal upset. It should be avoided by those sensitive to garlic.

POISONOUS LOOK-ALIKES: *Zigadenus spp.* (death camas) have similar grass-like leaves.

• Scent: Wild garlic has a distinctive garlic or onion smell when the leaves are crushed, whereas death camas does not.

• Flower: Wild garlic typically has pink to white flowers forming an umbel-like cluster. death camas often has creamy white to greenish-yellow flowers in a more elongated, spike-like cluster.

Zigadenus spp.

8 Ramps
Allium tricoccum

IDENTIFICATION FEATURES

STEM: Smooth green stems, often reddish near the base, giving rise to a single flowering stem per bulb cluster.

LEAF: 1 to 3 broad, elliptical leaves, 4-12 inches (10-30 cm) long and 1-3 inches (2.5-7.6 cm) wide, light green with possible purple or burgundy tints near the stem.

FLOWER: Small white flowers, less than an inch (2.5 cm) in size, grouped in clusters. Each flower has 3 sepals, 3 slightly longer petals, and 6 stamens with a single white style.

FRUIT: Three-lobed, green capsules that open via three valves, revealing round, black, shiny seeds.

BULB: White ovoid-conical bulbs, 0.8-2.4 inches (2-6 cm) long, surrounded by brownish-gray sheathing, usually forming clusters of 2-6 bulbs.

EDIBLE USE: The plant is edible and has a pungent garlic/onion flavor that is high in vitamin C. The bulbs and leaves can be used raw in salads or cooked in various dishes. They make an excellent base for soups, stir-fries, omelets, sandwiches, and egg dishes, and can also be pickled for longer storage. The leaves make a fantastic pesto and can be used in any recipe that calls for garlic or onions.

MEDICINAL USE: It has been used to treat colds, croup, and earaches, and as a springtime health tonic. It's considered a milder version of garlic in medicinal terms.

HARVESTING: The best time to harvest is in the spring, from March to June. Harvest sustainably by leaving some bulbs and leaves in the ground to allow the plant to regenerate.

CAUTION: It may cause allergic reactions or digestive problems if sensitive to onion or garlic. The plant may also interact with medications such as blood thinners or antibiotics.

POISONOUS LOOK-ALIKES: *Convallaria majalis* (lily-of-the-valley) has similar leaf shapes, and may grow in similar habitats.

• Ramps: Garlic or onion scent when crushed. Features 1-2 broad, smooth leaves per plant, with a cluster of white flowers.

• Lily-of-the-valley: Sweet scent, not oniony. Dark green leaves with parallel veins, and white, bell-shaped flowers on an unbranched stalk.

Convallaria majalis

OTHER NAMES: Lady's leek
HEIGHT: 1-2 feet (0.3-0.6 m) tall
HABITATS: Open woodlands, grasslands, mountains
EDIBLE PARTS: Bulb, leaves, flowers

9 Nodding Onion
Allium cernuum

IDENTIFICATION FEATURES

STEM: The stems are slender, smooth, and straight, round in cross-section, light green to reddish-green.

LEAF: The leaves are long, narrow, and grass-like, usually bending over near the top. They emerge from the base of the plant and are slightly shorter than the stem.

FLOWERS: The flowers are pink to lilac and form a downward-facing, or nodding, cluster at the top of the stem. Each flower is bell-shaped with 6 petal-like tepals, each 1/4 inch (0.6 cm) wide.

FRUITS: After flowering, the plant produces small, round, black seeds in a three-part capsule. Each capsule is about 1/8 inch (0.3 cm) across and contains one seed per valve.

BULB: It has a bulbous root system, typical of plants in the onion family. The bulb is small and covered with thin, papery skin.

ODOR: Nodding onion has a distinct onion or garlic-like smell when its leaves or bulbs are crushed.

EDIBLE USE: The bulb, leaves, and flowers are all edible. The bulbs, when cooked, offer a savory onion flavor, ideal for roasting, stewing, or adding to stir-fries. The slender, hollow leaves can be chopped and used fresh as a garnish or cooked into soups and stews, imparting a mild garlicky-onion flavor. The flower heads are also edible, adding oniony taste and visual appeal to salads. In addition, they can be pickled for a tangy treat.

MEDICINAL USE: Used as a poultice for respiratory ailments, for treating kidney stones, colds, croup, and sore throats.

HARVESTING: Nodding onion can be harvested from spring to fall. When harvesting, ensure to pick fresh, firm bulbs, leaves, and flowers. The bulb can be dug up from the ground, and the leaves and flowers can be snipped off.

CAUTION: While Nodding onion is edible and has medicinal properties, it is recommended that dogs should not consume large amounts as it can lead to poisoning.

POISONOUS LOOK-ALIKES: This plant could be confused with poisonous *Zigadenus spp.* (death camas). See descriptions on page 38.

10 Pawpaw
Asimina triloba

IDENTIFICATION FEATURES

BARK: Thin and smooth on young trees, becoming furrowed with age. It's typically light gray to brown.

BRANCHES: Slender and spreading, with a deep brown color. Twigs are light brown, and buds are dark brown and velvety.

LEAF: Simple, alternate, lance-shaped leaves; 5-12 inches (13-30 cm) long and 2-5 inches (5-13 cm) wide; dark green color on the upper surface and lighter green on the lower surface; leaves turn yellow in the fall. Disagreeable odor when bruised.

FLOWER: Maroon or dark brown; about 1-2 inches (2.5-5 cm) in diameter; have three sepals and six petals; often hidden beneath the foliage.

FRUIT: A large, oval, or oblong fruit; 2-6 inches (5-15 cm) in length and 1-3 inches (2.5-7.6 cm) in diameter; skin is thin and green, turning yellowish-green when ripe; encloses a soft, custard-like, aromatic, yellow-orange pulp.

SEED: Several large, flat, brown seeds within the fruit. 0.5-1 inch (1.2-2.5 cm) in diameter.

ODOR: Disagreeable when leaves and bark are bruised. Flowers have a faint fetid or yeasty smell.

EDIBLE USE: Pawpaw provides large, custard-like fruits that are sweet and aromatic. These fruits can be enjoyed fresh or used in various culinary applications such as smoothies, ice creams, cakes, muffins, and jams. The flavor is often likened to a banana, mango, and melon mix. Ripe pawpaws can also be frozen for later use. It's important to note that the skin and seeds of pawpaw fruits are not edible.

MEDICINAL USE: It has been used traditionally for its antioxidant properties, digestive health benefits, skincare applications, immune boosting, and potential anti-cancer effects. Scientific validation for these uses may vary.

HARVESTING: The best time to pick Pawpaw fruit is when its skin starts to turn from green to yellow, and the fruit yields slightly when squeezed. To harvest, gently twist the fruit from the tree or collect fallen fruit from the ground.

CAUTION: Unripe fruit, seeds, and other plant parts may be toxic if ingested. Always consume the fruit when it is fully ripe and discard the seeds.

OTHER NAMES: Longstyle sweet-cicely, sweet root, sweet anise, sweet chervil

HEIGHT: 2-3 feet (0.6-0.9 m) tall

HABITATS: Rich woods, wooded slopes, wooded ravines, and valleys.

EDIBLE PARTS: Green seeds, leaves, stems, flowers, roots

11 Aniseroot
Osmorhiza longistylis

IDENTIFICATION FEATURES

STEM: Stems are smooth to lightly hairy, becoming more hairy towards the top.

LEAF: Compound leaves, alternately arranged and singly or doubly grouped in threes, can grow up to 4 inches (10 cm) long and 2 inches (5 cm) wide. They feature shallow to deep lobes and toothed edges, and can be smooth or sparsely hairy.

FLOWER: Small, 1/8 inch (3 mm) white flowers, with five notched petals, five white-tipped stamens, and two white styles longer than the petals. The flowers form in flat clusters, or umbels, atop the plant and at the ends of the stems.

FRUIT: Fruits are slightly arced, narrow seeds about an inch (2.5 cm) long, covered in hairs, and mildly swollen at the tip.

ODOR: The crushed plant has a distinct anise scent.

EDIBLE USE: The roots have a strong anise scent and taste somewhat like licorice. They can be cut into small segments and used as a substitute for fennel seeds in cooking or baking. The leaves and stems are also edible and can be added to salads or soups for a mild anise flavor. The flowers can be used as a garnish or eaten raw. The young, green seeds, which are the tastiest part, are often used as a natural sweetener. They can be eaten raw, added to desserts or salads, or used to flavor liqueurs and other beverages.

MEDICINAL USE: Widely used by Native Americans as a remedy for various ailments such as wounds, boils, and digestive issues.

HARVESTING: The best time to pick the plant is in spring and summer when the leaves and flowers are young and tender. The roots can be harvested anytime, but they are more aromatic in autumn. To harvest the plant, dig up the roots carefully with a trowel or a knife, wash them well, and cut them into small pieces. The leaves and flowers can be picked by hand or with scissors.

CAUTION: It may cause allergic reactions in some people. It may also interact with medications such as anticoagulants or blood thinners. Avoid plants collected from polluted areas or sprayed with pesticides or herbicides.

POISONOUS LOOK-ALIKES: *Conium maculatum* (poison hemlock), *Cicuta spp.*(water hemlock) (See descriptions on page 43) have similar leaves and flowers to aniseroot. Always check for the anise-scented roots to confirm identification.

Notable Toxic Species in the Carrot Family

The Apiaceae (carrot family), includes some of the most lethal poisonous plants to humans. This vast family stands out with its signature umbrella-shaped flower clusters, or umbels, and frequently aromatic leaves. Plants 11-14 fall under this family, and they closely resemble the dangerous look-alikes listed below. Extreme caution is crucial when coming across these plants in nature. Familiarize yourself with their distinct characteristics to guarantee correct identification before consuming any wild member of the carrot family.

Conium maculatum

Conium maculatum (POISON HEMLOCK): Contains toxic alkaloids that can be lethal. This plant is famously associated with the death of the philosopher Socrates.
- Tall, often reaching 6 to 10 feet.
- Smooth, green stems distinctly mottled with reddish-purple.
- Delicate, fern-like leaves.
- White umbrella-shaped flower clusters.
- Odor: Unpleasant, mousy or musty odor, especially when crushed.

Cicuta spp.

Cicuta spp. (WATER HEMLOCK): Contains cicutoxin, primarily in roots. Ingestion causes seizures and can be fatal.
- Stout, hollow stems with clear or yellowish aromatic liquid.
- Small, green or white umbrella-shaped flower clusters.
- Feathery, double or triple pinnate leaves.
- Found near water sources like swamps or streambanks.
- Odor: Characteristic parsnip-like smell.

Heracleum mantegazzianum

Heracleum mantegazzianum (GIANT HOGWEED): Sap causes severe skin burns upon exposure to sunlight, leading to blisters and scars.
- Huge, deeply lobed leaves, sometimes over 5 feet across.
- Thick, bristly stalks reaching over 12 feet with purple blotches.
- Large white, umbrella-shaped flower clusters.
- Odor: Slightly unpleasant, acrid scent.

General Information
OTHER NAMES: Golden zizia
HEIGHT: 16-30 inches (40-76 cm) tall
HABITATS: Moist woods, meadows, thickets, prairies, and overgrown urban lots
EDIBLE PARTS: Flowers

being stalkless.

FRUIT: The green fruit capsules are oblong and 0.12-0.16 inches (3-4 mm) long. As fall progresses, they turn a light purple color. Each fruit contains two seeds.

EDIBLE USE: Flowers of the plant are edible. These bright yellow blossoms can be added to salads, offering a vibrant visual appeal and a subtle, unique flavor. When cooked, they hint at the taste of broccoli. For a culinary twist, they can be sautéed in a light butter-garlic sauce, creating a delightful side dish or garnish for main courses.

MEDICINAL USE: Used medicinally as a root tea to reduce fever. Additionally, the root is believed to have wound healing and hypnotic properties.

HARVESTING: The best time to pick *Zizia aurea* in the wild is in late spring or summer when the flowers bloom. It can be harvested by gently plucking the flowers to retain their delicate structure.

CAUTION: It may cause allergic reactions in some people. The root may be toxic if consumed in large quantities. It may interact with some medications, such as sedatives or blood thinners.

POISONOUS LOOK-ALIKES: *Conium maculatum* (poison hemlock), *Cicuta spp.* (water hemlock) (See descriptions on page 43) have similar leaves and flowers structure. Always check for the bright yellow flowers to confirm identification.

12 Golden Alexanders
Zizia aurea

IDENTIFICATION FEATURES

STEM: Sturdy stems that are green or purple.

LEAF: Compound and measure up to 3 inches (8 cm) long and 2 inches (5 cm) wide. They are attached alternately to the stem. Each leaflet is usually spear-shaped or egg-shaped with serrated edges. In fall, these green leaves gradually transition to a light purple hue.

FLOWER: The yellow flowers are less than 0.12 inches (3 mm) long, each featuring five sepals, petals, and stamens. They grow in flat-topped umbels, or clusters, at the top of the plant, with the middle flower of each umbel

13 Great Angelica
Angelica atropurpurea

IDENTIFICATION FEATURES

STEM: Thick, hollow, and purplish at the base.

LEAF: The leaves are large, up to 2 feet (0.6 m) long, and compound, with each leaf divided into multiple leaflets. Each leaflet is broad, ovate (egg-shaped), 0.75–4.5 inches (1.9–11.4 cm) long, toothed on the edges, and arranged alternately along the stem. They are rich, deep green.

FLOWER: The flowers are small, greenish-white to pale pink, and appear in large, rounded, umbrella-like clusters (umbels) that can reach up to 8 inches (20.3 cm) across.

FRUIT: After flowering, the plant produces small, oblong, ribbed fruits that turn from green to brown as they mature.

SEED: The seeds are small, oblong, and ridged, with a light brown color.

ROOT: The root is thick, fleshy, and branched, with a dark brown exterior and lighter interior. It has a strong, distinctive aroma and is traditionally used in herbal medicine.

EDIBLE USE: The plant has been used as a flavoring agent in various dishes. The young shoots and leaves can be cooked and used in soups, stews, and other dishes. The stems, when peeled, can be candied and are often used in confectionery or as a flavoring agent in various dishes. The roots can be utilized as a unique flavoring in crafting homemade liqueurs, adding a distinct aromatic profile prized in various traditional concoctions.

MEDICINAL USE: It is known for digestive aid properties; it can also be used for menstrual and respiratory issues. Externally, it can be applied to skin conditions like psoriasis and eczema.

HARVESTING: The best time to harvest great angelica is in the spring when the young leaves and stems are tender. Carefully cut the leaves and stems near the base of the plant. The roots can be dug up in the fall, after the plant has finished flowering and the foliage begins to die back.

CAUTION: Some people may have an allergic reaction to the plant, particularly if they are sensitive to other plants in the carrot family, such as carrots, celery, or parsnip.

POISONOUS LOOK-ALIKES: Great angelica closely resembles several poisonous plants in the carrot family, such as *Heracleum mantegazzianum* (giant hogweed). See descriptions on page 43.

General Information

OTHER NAMES: Florence fennel, finocchio

HEIGHT: Up to 8 feet (2.5 m) tall

HABITATS: Coastal areas, riverbanks, roadsides, fields, and disturbed areas

EDIBLE PARTS: Roots, young leaves, stems, and fruits

14 Fennel
Foeniculum vulgare

IDENTIFICATION FEATURES

STEM: Hollow stems that are straight, grooved, and glaucous green.

LEAF: The bright green leaves are finely divided into thread-like segments, giving a feathery appearance.

FLOWER: The flowers are small, yellow and grow in flat-topped clusters called umbels, which can contain up to 50 individual flowers. These clusters can be up to 6 inches (15 cm) across and are held high above the foliage on the tall stems.

FRUITS: The fruits are oblong and grooved. They're green when young, turning gray as they mature. The fruits are commonly referred to as fennel "seeds" due to their small size and seed-like appearance.

ODOR: Fennel is highly aromatic, with a scent that is similar to anise or licorice.

EDIBLE USE: The roots can be used in various ways, including sautéing, stewing, grilling, or braising. The tender leaves and stems, which have a subtle taste, serve as garnishes or are added to salads, sauces, and soups to enhance flavor. The fruits, typically referred to as seeds, are used as a spice and provide a distinctive anise-like aroma. These seeds are crucial in an array of dishes, from Indian cuisine to Mediterranean salads, and are notably used in Italian sausage for its specific flavor.

MEDICINAL USE: Fennel is used for digestive issues like indigestion and stomach pains. The seeds are the most active part, and essential oil from the seeds is used in aromatherapy for its normalizing, bactericidal, and stimulant properties.

HARVESTING: Fennel can be harvested throughout its growth stages. The young leaves can be picked as needed, and the root can be harvested year round. The seeds are best harvested when they turn brown. They should be dried and kept in an airtight container in a dark, dry place.

CAUTION: Avoid consuming large amounts due to its potent essential oil. Pregnant women should avoid the essential oil and concentrated forms of fennel.

POISONOUS LOOK-ALIKES: *Conium maculatum* (poison hemlock) (See descriptions on page 43) have similar appearances. Always check for a strong aniseed scent to confirm identification.

15 Common Milkweed
Asclepias syriaca

IDENTIFICATION FEATURES

STEM: Thick stems in light green or reddish hues that exude milky sap when crushed.

LEAVES: Light green, broadly oval-shaped to oblong leaves (4-11 inches or 10–28 cm long) with a central vein and smooth edges. They produces a milky sap when crushed.

FLOWER: Small pink to purplish blooms in umbrella-like clusters, featuring five downward-pointing petals (reflexed petals) and a crown-like structure at the center composed of five upright hoods, each containing a small horn.

FRUIT: A warty, spindle-shaped pod (2-4 inches or 5-10 cm long) that turns brown upon drying and releases flat, oval seeds with white, fluffy tufts.

ODOR: A pleasant aroma reminiscent of vanilla, most prominent in flower clusters.

EDIBLE USE: Young shoots can be cooked like asparagus. Flower buds and young leaves can be used as substitutes for broccoli and spinach, respectively, with a distinct sweet, pea-like flavor. Buds can make a sugary syrup. Young pods taste like okra and seeds, when boiled and strained, add a cheese-like texture and mild flavor to dishes. The plant's latex, mixed with animal fat, was a chewing gum alternative.

MEDICINAL USE: Roots and latex offer relief for ailments like asthma and kidney stones and possess expectorant, diaphoretic, and purgative properties.

HARVESTING: Harvest young shoots by snapping off an inch above the ground. Pinch off the green flower heads and cook as desired. Harvest young firm pods when they are under 1.5 inches (3.8 cm) long. Pull out the seed fibers when the pods are beginning to lose firmness but are still green.

CAUTION: Older plant parts contain cardiac glycosides, posing risks to humans and animals. Some might be sensitive to milkweed, so it's advisable to try a small amount first.

POISONOUS LOOK-ALIKES: *Apocynum cannabinum* (dogbane) is highly toxic.

• dogbane features narrower leaves and smaller greenish-white flowers.

• dogbane stems are reddish-brown with a more branching growth pattern than the straighter-stemmed milkweed.

• dogbane has a bitter taste.

Apocynum cannabinum

16 Wild Sarsaparilla
Aralia nudicaulis

IDENTIFICATION FEATURES

STEM: The stem is typically light green to brownish-red and smooth.

LEAF: The leaves are large and compound, typically made up of 3 groups of 3 to 7 leaflets each. They are oval to round in shape, 3 to 5 inches (7.6-12.7 cm) long, with a serrated edge and a pointed tip.

FLOWER: The flowers are small, greenish-white to white, about 1/8 inch (3 mm) across, and appear in round clusters on separate stalks from the leafy stems. Each flower cluster may have up to 40 individual flowers.

FRUIT: The fruits are small berries, initially green, but turn dark purple to black when ripe. Each fruit contains up to 5 seeds.

ROOT: The plant has a thick, aromatic, and horizontal root that grows just below the surface of the ground.

EDIBLE USE: Its young shoots are harvested in the spring and can be cooked and consumed as a potherb, adding an interesting component to stir-fries, soups, or stews. Additionally, the aromatic root of the plant can be boiled to make a root beer-like beverage, while its

General Information

OTHER NAMES: Shot bush, small spikenard, wild liquorice, rabbit root

HEIGHT: 12-24 inches (30–60 cm) tall

HABITATS: Shaded woodlands and forest understories

EDIBLE PARTS: Roots, young shoots, fruit

dark berries, although not particularly tasty on their own, can be transformed into a type of jelly or used as a flavoring agent in other recipes.

MEDICINAL USE: Wild sarsaparilla is a healing herb that can help with sweating, urine production, lung health, and energy boost. It's used for issues like lung diseases, asthma, and skin problems.

HARVESTING: The root of the wild sarsaparilla is harvested in late summer and fall. The roots are dug up, cleaned, and dried for later use. The young shoots are collected in the spring when tender, and the fruit is gathered when ripe.

CAUTION: Wild sarsaparilla can cause allergic reactions in some people. Always consult a healthcare professional before use, particularly if you are pregnant, breastfeeding, or have chronic health conditions.

OTHER NAMES: Garden asparagus, sparrow grass

HEIGHT: 40-60 inches (1-1.5 m) tall

HABITATS: Beaches, and marsh edges

EDIBLE PARTS: Young shoots (spears)

17 Asparagus
Asparagus officinalis

IDENTIFICATION FEATURES

STEM: Stems are usually straight, green, or purple, and have triangular bracts. They start thick and stand upright but become thin and multi-branched as they mature.

LEAF: The plant's "leaves" are modified stems known as cladodes. These cladodes are soft, feathery, and needle-like, grouped in clusters resembling a rose shape.

FLOWER: Petite and bell-shaped, exhibiting hues from greenish-white to yellowish. Each flower comprises six tepals that are partially fused at the base. The flowers are singly or in clusters of two to three at the junctions of the branchlets.

FRUIT: The fruit is a small, hard, shiny, red berry, measuring 0.24-0.4 inches (6-10 mm) in diameter. These berries are toxic to humans.

EDIBLE USE: The young shoots are typically harvested and cooked in various ways, including steaming, boiling, roasting, or grilling. They can be served as a standalone side dish, often with sea salt, olive oil, and a squeeze of lemon. Alternatively, they can be incorporated into a variety of dishes, such as stir-fries, pasta dishes, and salads. The asparagus tips, in particular, are considered delicacies and often highlighted in dishes. Asparagus is also commonly used in soups, and its unique, earthy flavor can also be used to create sauces.

MEDICINAL USE: Asparagus acts as a diuretic, anti-inflammatory, anti-rheumatic, and laxative. It can help treat urinary tract infections, kidney stones, constipation, and edema. Additionally, it can lower blood pressure and cholesterol levels and improve liver and kidney function.

HARVESTING: Young shoots are ideally picked in spring when they reach 6-8 inches in height. Cut stems at the base with a sharp knife, not harming the plant's crown to allow for future growth. The entire plant can be relocated to your own garden for personal cultivation.

CAUTION: It may cause allergic reactions or digestive issues in some people, can affect urine smell and color.

General Information

OTHER NAMES: False spikenard
HEIGHT: 2-3 feet (0.6-0.9 m) tall
HABITATS: Moist, rich woods and forests, thickets, stream banks, and slopes
EDIBLE PARTS: Young shoots, berries, roots

18 False Solomon's Seal
Maianthemum racemosum

IDENTIFICATION FEATURES

STEM: Single, unbranched, and presents an arching form.

LEAF: Light green, long, wider in the middle, and tapering to pointed ends, arranged alternately along the stem. They are 3-6 inches (7-15 cm) long and 1.2-2.4 inches (3-6 cm) wide. The base of each leaf rounds off or narrows down, while the leaf tips are pointy and sometimes a bit extended.

FLOWER: Small, creamy white flowers that are star-shaped and less than 1 inch (2.4 cm) in diameter. These flowers are arranged in clusters containing up to 80 individual flowers, each with six tepals.

FRUIT: Start off as green with copper spots and mature to a ruby red color by late summer. The fruits are round to 3-lobed and contain a few seeds.

EDIBLE USE: The young shoots and berries can be consumed. The young shoots are best harvested in the spring and boiled and eaten as a vegetable, similar to asparagus. They have a mild, sweet flavor and can be used in a variety of dishes, including stir-fries, soups, and stews. The ripe berries, which turn a bright red in the late summer, can be eaten raw or cooked. They can be used in jams, jellies, pies, or any other dish that calls for berries. The roots are also edible when leached.

MEDICINAL USE: The leaf or root can be crushed and used to soothe skin irritations like scrapes and rashes, and a root tea is gargled for oral discomforts like sore throats.

HARVESTING: Young shoots can be snapped off at the base of the stem. The berries can be harvested when they have turned a ruby red color.

CAUTION: Eating large quantities of berries can cause diarrhea.

POISONOUS LOOK-ALIKES: True solomon's seal (*Polygonatum spp.*) berries are mildly toxic.

• Flowers & Fruits: *M. racemosum* has a plume of small, starry flowers at the tip that turns into speckled red berries, while *Polygonatum spp.* have bell-shaped flowers (and later, blue-black berries) hanging from the leaf axils along the stem.

• Stem: *Polygonatum*'s stem is more arching, while *M. racemosum*'s stem is straighter.

Polygonatum spp. (poisonous berries)

OTHER NAMES: Sunroot, sunchoke, earth apple

HEIGHT: 5-10 feet (1.5 to 3 m) tall

HABITATS: Prairies, plains, woodlands, riverbanks, roadsides, and gardens

EDIBLE PARTS: Tubers

19 Jerusalem Artichoke
Helianthus tuberosus

IDENTIFICATION FEATURES

STEM: Rough, hairy, and often branches near the top. It displays a green to red/burgundy color and has a round cross-section.

LEAF: Arranged alternately at the top and oppositely towards the bottom. Lower leaves are broadly oval and pointed and can be up to 12 inches (30 cm) long, while upper leaves are usually smaller and narrower.

FLOWER: Yellow capitate flowerheads, 2-4 inches (5-10 cm) in diameter, with 10-20 ray florets and numerous small disc florets. They give off a brief, light, vanilla-chocolate fragrance.

FRUIT: Brown or copper-colored and ripens during the fall. The seeds can serve as a food source for various birds.

TUBER: Long and irregular, similar to a ginger root. Its texture is crisp and crunchy. Colors can range from pale brown to white, red, or purple.

EDIBLE USE: The tubers can be eaten raw or cooked. Raw, they add a crunchy texture to salads and have a sweet, nutty flavor. Cooked, they can be used the same way as potatoes - boiled, baked, roasted, or fried. They can be turned into a creamy soup, roasted with herbs and spices as a side dish, or used as the base for a gratin. The tubers are also used to make various fermented products, including a unique type of beer. They are rich in carbohydrates, especially inulin, a type of fiber that can benefit digestion and blood sugar levels.

MEDICINAL USE: Traditionally used to help with digestion, stimulate urine production, and support sperm production. It also acts as a general health tonic. Furthermore, it has been used in folk medicine to treat diabetes and rheumatism.

HARVESTING: The tubers are best harvested from late fall onwards, following the first frost which enhances flavor and sweetness by converting inulin to fructose. Carefully dig them up using a fork or spade, considering their irregular shape and fragility. Wash thoroughly and store in a cool, dry place.

CAUTION: Tubers contain inulin, which can cause gas and bloating in some people.

20 Canada lettuce
Lactuca canadensis

IDENTIFICATION FEATURES

STEM: Hairless and often has a waxy or powdery coating, light or reddish-green color, unbranched except in the flower clusters. When broken or cut, the stem exudes a distinctive milky latex sap.

LEAF: Alternately arranged, vary from deep pinnate lobes to no lobes. Color ranges from light to dark green, sometimes with purple or yellow casts. Slightly toothed with small hairs along underside veins.

FLOWER: Dandelion-like, yellowish or slightly red to orange, consists of 12-25 florets. Blooms in late summer or early fall, scentless.

FRUIT: Dark-colored achene about 0.2 inches (5 mm) long with a slightly flattened and curved white pappus, often with black

General Information

OTHER NAMES: Tall lettuce, Florida blue lettuce

HEIGHT: 20-79 inches (50 to 200 cm) tall

HABITATS: Forest edges, meadows, fields, roadsides, open woodlands, and disturbed areas

EDIBLE PARTS: Young leaves, stems

spots.

SEED: Brown, flattened, oval, possesses a long slender beak with a tuft of white hairs at the tip.

ROOT: Thick, deep taproot that contains white latex.

EDIBLE USE: The leaves and stems can be consumed. The leaves have a rich content of vitamins A, C, and K and calcium, iron, and potassium. They can be used in salads, adding a mild, slightly bitter flavor similar to cultivated lettuce. They can also be cooked and used in soups, stews, or stir-fries. The young stems can be peeled and consumed raw or cooked. They have a crisp texture and a mild flavor that complement a variety of dishes.

MEDICINAL USE: The sap of this plant is known for its analgesic, soothing, and antispasmodic properties. It's been used for treating various conditions, such as pain, insomnia, and respiratory ailments. It can be topically applied to treat skin issues. The leaves serve as a poultice for inflammation and wound healing.

HARVESTING: The optimal time for harvesting is spring to summer, before the plant flowers. Cut the stem near the base and collect the leaves.

CAUTION: Consuming the sap in large amounts can lead to side effects like nausea and hallucinations. It is not advised for pregnant or breastfeeding women, individuals allergic to latex or ragweed, or those on blood thinners or anticoagulants.

21 Sow Thistle
Sonchus oleraceus

IDENTIFICATION FEATURES

STEM: Upright, hollow, displaying a dull, waxy sheen.

LEAF: Deeply divided with triangular lobes, though upper leaves may be merely toothed or shallowly lobed. Lower leaves are long-stalked, and upper leaves are smaller. All leaves have a dull, waxy sheen and are coarsely toothed with small, soft prickles.

FLOWER: Yellow dandelion-like, 0.75-1.25 inches (1.9-3.2 cm) across. Appear in tight clusters at the top of the stem and from leaf axils.

FRUIT: Dark brown seed, slightly flattened, spindle-shaped with textured ribs and bright white hairs.

EDIBLE USE: The leaves, stems, and roots are edible. The leaves and stems are often eaten raw in salads, providing a crisp texture and a mildly bitter flavor. They can also be cooked and used in many dishes, including soups, stews, and stir-fries. The leaves are naturally high in vitamin C, iron, calcium, and potassium. The young roots are also edible and are used as a coffee substitute.

MEDICINAL USE: Traditionally, the plant serves various ailments such as ulcers, coughs, skin problems, and wounds. The sap treats topical conditions like warts, while leaves in tea or poultice form aid sore throats and kidney stones. The seeds act as a laxative or expectorant.

HARVESTING: Optimal in spring or summer when the plant is tender. Harvest involves cutting stems near the base or uprooting them. Thoroughly wash leaves before consumption or medicinal use.

CAUTION: Consumption from polluted soils or heavily fertilized areas may cause methemoglobinemia, leading to dizziness and nausea. It can also cause allergic reactions in those sensitive to the Aster family. Its coumarin content may increase bleeding risks when combined with blood-thinning medications.

General Information

OTHER NAMES: Common dandelion

HEIGHT: 2-16 inches (5-41 cm) tall

HABITATS: Lawns, gardens, meadows, fields, roadsides, waste places, forests, and mountains

EDIBLE PARTS: Leaves, flowers, roots

22 Dandelion
Taraxacum officinale

IDENTIFICATION FEATURES

STEM: The stem can show a purplish tint, stand upright or slack, hollow, unbranched, leafless. Either smooth or sparsely covered with short hairs. The stems produce milky sap.

LEAF: Elongated leaves, 2-18 inches (5-45 cm) long and 0.4-4 inches (1-10 cm) wide, taper towards the stalk, with jagged or toothed edges in a circular base arrangement.

FLOWER: Bright yellow flower heads, 0.6-1 inch (14–25 mm) wide, with each head containing 40 to over 100 individual florets. Each flower head is held on a stem as tall or taller than the leaves.

FRUIT: Shaped like a ball of tiny fruits called "cypselae". Each fruit is 0.08-0.12 inches (2–3 mm) long with a slender beak.

The silky pappi, which form the parachutes, are white to silver-white.

SEED: Fluffy, round seeds dispersed by wind, in shades of green, brown, or gray.

EDIBLE USE: The plant is edible from root to flower, and has been used as food for centuries. The leaves can be used in salads or cooked in similar ways to spinach. They have a bitter flavor that can be balanced with sweeter or richer ingredients. The young leaves are more tender and less bitter than the older ones. The flowers can be consumed raw or cooked as well, or used to make wine, tea, jelly, syrup, vinegar, or honey. The roots can be roasted and ground to make a coffee substitute or brewed as tea.

MEDICINAL USE: Traditionally used for ailments like digestive disorders, liver problems, and skin conditions. It has diuretic, tonic, and blood-purifying properties, with potential antioxidant, anti-inflammatory, and antimicrobial effects.

HARVESTING: The flowers can be picked anytime they are in bloom. Use a sharp tool to cut leaves and flowers at the stem base. For roots, dig around the plant and pull out the whole root. Always clean thoroughly before use.

CAUTION: Some people may experience allergic reactions or side effects like skin rashes or stomach upset. It may affect people with allergies to similar plants or those with gallstones or liver disease. It may also have interactions with medications like blood thinners, diuretics, lithium, or antibiotics.

OTHER NAMES: Oyster plant, Jerusalem star, Jack go to bed

HEIGHT: Up to 4 feet (1.2 m) tall

HABITATS: Roadsides, vacant lots, woodlands, and grasslands

EDIBLE PARTS: Young shoots, leaves, roots, flowers

23 Purple Salsify
Tragopogon porrifolius

IDENTIFICATION FEATURES

STEM: Light green, generally unbranched, and exude a sticky, milky sap when cut or torn.

LEAF: Long and thin, 8-15 inches (20-38 cm) long, resembling grass, light green and waxy or powdery on the underside, alternating along the stem.

FLOWER: A single purple flower head per stalk, 2-4 inches (5-10 cm) wide, daisy-like. The center consists of deep purple to black florets with yellow stigmas. The flower has eight long sepals, longer than the petals, and 1-2 circles of dark purple filaments with gold anthers.

FRUIT: Looks like a dandelion puffball, with seeds inside a tuft of white hair, aiding wind dispersal.

SEED: Tiny, brownish, found within the fruit's pappus.

ROOT: Taproot, thick and fleshy, 6-12 inches (15–30 cm) long. Tastes like oysters.

SAP: Milky and sticky, oozes from stems when cut or torn.

EDIBLE USE: The roots can be boiled, roasted, or steamed and have a unique flavor that is often compared to oysters, hence its common name. They can be mashed, or sliced and added to soups and stews. The roots can also be used in stir-fries or grated raw into salads.

The young shoots and leaves of the plant can also be eaten, either raw in salads or cooked similarly to other green vegetables. They offer a slightly bitter taste that can complement a variety of dishes. The flowers are also edible.

MEDICINAL USE: Traditionally used for liver and gallbladder issues, constipation, and skin diseases, it is reported to possess diuretic, laxative, anti-inflammatory, and tonic properties.

HARVESTING: Ideally, harvest young shoots and leaves in spring or summer and mature, flavorful roots in the second year's fall or winter. Use a sharp tool to cut or dig up the desired parts and wash thoroughly before consumption or storage.

CAUTION: Generally safe in moderate quantities, *Tragopogon porrifolius* may cause allergic or digestive reactions in some individuals.

24 Chicory
Cichorium intybus

IDENTIFICATION FEATURES

STEM: Tough, grooved, with hair, color from green to reddish-brown. The bottom part often has hairs, with milky sap inside.

LEAF: Stalked, lance-shaped, without lobes, 3-12.6 inches (7.5-32 cm) long and 0.8-3.1 inches (2-8 cm) wide. Smaller on top, alternate on the stem. Leaf margins can be lobed, toothed, or smooth. Typically hairy along the midrib underneath.

FLOWER: The flower heads are 1-1.5 inches (2.5-3.8 cm) wide with numerous bright blue rays with blunt-toothed edges. They attach directly to the stem, open in the morning, and close by noon unless it is cloudy.

FRUIT: The fruit is a brown oblong and 5-ribbed achene with blunt ends. The wider end has bristles across the top.

SEED: Encased within the achene, the seed has small scales at the tip.

SAP: Milky, contained within the stem.

EDIBLE USE: The leaves can be consumed raw in salads, providing a slightly bitter flavor that can balance out sweeter or richer ingredients. They can also be cooked and used in various dishes, including soups, stews, and stir-fries.

General Information

OTHER NAMES: Blue daisy, coffeeweed

HEIGHT: Can grow up to 5 feet (1.5 m) tall

HABITATS: Roadsides, railroads, disturbed sites or waste ground

EDIBLE PARTS: Leaves, roots, flowers

The plant's roots can be roasted and ground to make a coffee substitute or additive, offering a unique, slightly bitter flavor. They can also be boiled or roasted and eaten as a vegetable. The flowers, while somewhat bitter, can be used to garnish salads and other dishes.

MEDICINAL USE: Traditionally, chicory roots have been used to alleviate symptoms associated with mild digestive disorders, such as abdominal fullness, flatulence, slow digestion, and temporary loss of appetite.

HARVESTING: Chicory is a perennial plants that flowers from May until the first frost in the fall. The leaves are harvested as the plant begins to bloom and can be dried for later use. The root can be consumed fresh or dried, and can be harvested in the fall or early spring.

CAUTION: Some people may experience skin irritation from contact with the plant, or digestive upset if consumed in large quantities.

25 Common Burdock
Arctium minus

IDENTIFICATION FEATURES

STEM: Green or reddish-green, stout, smooth with long veins. It's round or slightly ridged. Young stems can be covered in white hairs.

LEAF: Broad, heart-shaped leaves resemble elephant's ears with rounded tips and long, hollow stalks. With wavy edges, these leaves can reach sizes up to 2 feet (0.6 m) long and over a foot (0.3 m) in width. They become smaller, lack stalks, and are less wavy near the flower clusters. Display a dense, hairy texture and alternate in arrangement.

FLOWER: Pink to purple, about 0.75-1 inch (1.9-2.5 cm) wide, on stalks. Made up of many disk florets and thin, sharp-tipped bracts. No ray florets.

FRUIT: Brown or copper, oblong-shaped achene, less than 1 inch (2.5 cm) long. It has fine bristles at one end that can float in the air and cause irritation.

ROOT: Very deep, up to 12 inches (30 cm), with brown peel and white inside in a cone shape.

EDIBLE USE: The roots, stems, flower stalks, and leaves are edible. Burdock roots are the tastiest; they can be boiled, roasted, or steamed and are often used in Asian cuisine, particularly in Japan, where it is known as "gobo". The roots have a sweet, earthy flavor and can be used in many dishes, from stir-fries to soups and stews. Younger plant stems and flower stalks are edible until they turn woody and bitter. After removing the tough outer layer, the slender inner stem can be cooked like asparagus or added raw to salads. The leaves can also be cooked, though they have a bitter flavor.

MEDICINAL USE: The roots and leaves of burdock are traditionally used for treating colds, gout, stomach issues, and cancers. It also promotes urination, increases sweating, and aids bowel movements.

HARVESTING: The central stalk can be harvested only during a small window in the early summer, while the leaf stalks can be harvested throughout the year. The best time to harvest first-year roots is by late fall, though you can harvest until flowers appear in the second year.

CAUTION: Burs and bristles may cause severe eye, skin, or respiratory problems. Burs can be difficult to get out of animal fur and clothing.

General Information

OTHER NAMES: Milk thistle, compass plant, scarole.

HEIGHT: Up to 6.6 feet (2 m) tall

HABITATS: Roadsides, fields, gardens, and waste places

EDIBLE PARTS: Young leaves, stems, seeds

26 Prickly Lettuce
Lactuca serriola

IDENTIFICATION FEATURES

STEM: The stem is erect, leafy, and hollow, with a milky sap that exudes when cut.

LEAF: The leaves are alternate, oblong, and deeply lobed, with prickles on the margins and midrib. The lower leaves are larger and more divided than the upper ones. When cut open, a latex substance comes out.

FLOWER: The flowers are yellow, 0.4-0.6 inch (1-1.5 cm) wide, and arranged in loose clusters at the ends of the branches. There are 12-20 ray flowers but no disc flowers. The flowers bloom from July to September.

FRUIT: The fruits are brown, ribbed, and cylindrical seeds, with a tuft of white hairs at the tip.

EDIBLE USE: The young leaves can be used in salads or cooked like spinach, while the mature leaves can be boiled to reduce their bitterness before being added to soups or stews. The stems, if harvested before they become too fibrous, can be peeled, boiled, and eaten like asparagus or celery. They can also be pickled for long-term storage. The plant's seeds can be pressed to extract an edible oil for cooking or as a salad dressing.

MEDICINAL USE: The plant's milky sap can soothe pain and aid sleep. It's been traditionally used for problems like insomnia, anxiety, stomach issues, and urinary infections.

HARVESTING: The optimal time to harvest its young, tender leaves is before the plant bolts, as bolting can make the leaves bitter. By late spring or early fall, the mature seed heads can be collected. When harvesting, use garden shears for the leaves and pluck dried seed heads by hand. Wear gloves, as the plant's milky sap can irritate some people's skin.

CAUTION: Use carefully and with professional guidance as it can cause drowsiness in normal amounts and potentially heart issues in large amounts. The mature plant can be mildly toxic, and cause stomach upsets if eaten in large amounts.

OTHER NAMES: Old man's pepper, devil's nettle, sanguinary, milfoil

HEIGHT: 1-3 feet (0.3-0.9 m) tall

HABITATS: Grasslands, meadows, open woodlands, and along roadsides

EDIBLE PARTS: Young leaves

27 Yarrow
Achillea millefolium

IDENTIFICATION FEATURES

STEM: The stem is erect, generally unbranched, and covered in fine hairs. It can grow up to 3 feet (90 cm) in height and has a strong aromatic scent.

LEAF: The leaves are alternate and feather-like, giving them a fern-like appearance. They are usually a bright green color, though they can vary, and are covered in fine hairs. Has a strong spicy aroma.

FLOWER: Flowers are small and appear in flat, round clusters (corymbs) at the top of the stem. They are generally white or pale pink, each with 3 to 8 ray florets around a center of numerous tiny disc florets. Blooms from April to September.

FRUIT: Small, dry, one-seeded fruits called cypsela, oblong and slightly curved.

SEED: The seeds are tiny, brown, and oblong in shape.

ODOR: Distinctive, strong, and somewhat sweet scent

EDIBLE USE: Yarrow has leaves that can be consumed raw or cooked. They have a somewhat bitter taste but can be used in small amounts in salads and soups for their aromatic, herbaceous flavor. The leaves can also be used as a seasoning, similar to how one might use sage. Historically, the plant has been used in brewing beer as a flavoring and preservative.

MEDICINAL USE: It has been used for wound healing, treatment of fevers and colds, digestive disorders, and as a mild sedative. It's also applied topically for skin conditions.

HARVESTING: The best time to harvest yarrow is when the leaves are young and tender, and the flowers are just beginning to bloom. Carefully snip the leaves and flower clusters from the plant using a pair of scissors or a sharp knife.

CAUTION: Yarrow is generally safe in moderation, but large quantities may cause allergies or gastrointestinal upset. Pregnant or nursing women should avoid it due to potential uterine contractions.

28 Tarragon
Artemisia dracunculus

IDENTIFICATION FEATURES

STEM: Tarragon has upright, branched stems reaching 2-4 feet (0.6-1.2 m). The stems are slender, smooth and become woody with age. They are typically green but can also have a reddish tinge.

LEAF: The leaves are linear to narrowly lance-shaped and glossy green. They typically measure 1-4 inches (2.5-10 cm) long and are arranged alternately along the stem. The leaves have smooth margins and a distinctive aroma.

FLOWER: The flowers are small, yel-

General Information

OTHER NAMES: Estragon, dragon plant

HEIGHT: 4-5 feet (1.2-1.5 m) tall

HABITATS: Roadsides, meadows, desert scrub habitats, and disturbed areas

EDIBLE PARTS: Leaves, shoots

low-green, and arranged in rounded clusters called panicles. Each cluster consists of many individual flowers that bloom from July to November.

FRUIT: Tarragon's fruit is a small, hard nutlet. It is typically propagated through root division or stem cuttings.

ODOR: The wild tarragon variety has a minimal fragrance. Cultivated varieties used for culinary purposes are more pungent and flavorful.

EDIBLE USE: Tarragon plays a vital role in various culinary traditions. Fresh tarragon leaves are often used in salads, soups, sauces and as a flavoring for vinegar. They are common in French dishes, notably in Béarnaise sauce, a classic French sauce that pairs well with steak. Tarragon also complements fish, chicken, and egg dishes. Its leaves can be used to infuse oils and butter or can be dried for long-term storage. Tarragon's distinct, slightly sweet anise flavor adds a unique touch to a wide range of dishes.

MEDICINAL USE: Has been used traditionally for its digestive, diuretic, and sedative properties. It has also been used to alleviate toothaches and as an appetite stimulant.

HARVESTING: The best time to harvest Tarragon leaves is in the morning, after the dew has evaporated but before the heat of the day. Cut the stems just above a set of leaves or at the base of the plant. Tarragon can be harvested throughout the growing season.

General Information

HEIGHT: Up to 31 inches (80 cm) tall

HABITATS: Mountain forests, grassland, and desert scrub

EDIBLE PARTS: Leaves, roots, seeds, young shoots, stem

29 Arrowleaf Balsamroot
Balsamorhiza sagittata

IDENTIFICATION FEATURES

STEM: The stem is typically short and stout, covered in small hairs and glands, emerging directly from a basal rosette.

LEAF: The leaves are large, up to 20 inches (50 cm) long, arrowhead-shaped (sagittate), and have a rough texture with hairs on both sides. They are basal, forming a rosette at the ground level. The leaves are green on the upper surface and white or grayish on the lower surface due to a dense layer of hair.

FLOWER: Large, showy, and daisy-like, typically 4 inches (10 cm) wide. They feature bright yellow petals surrounding a darker yellow or brownish central disc. This central disc consists of many small florets.

FRUIT: The fruits are small and dry achenes and do not open to release the seeds when mature.

SEED: The seeds are small, with a tuft of hairs attached, similar to dandelion seeds.

ROOT: Large, woody taproot that extends deep into the soil.

ODOR: The plant has a distinctive, pleasant scent, especially when the leaves or roots are crushed.

EDIBLE USE: The root, characterized by its balsamic aroma, can be cooked and eaten. It is typically slow-roasted or boiled. The roasted root are used as a coffee substitute.

Additionally, the young shoots, flowering stems and leaves can be consumed either raw or cooked, offering a crisp texture and a mildly bitter taste. These can be a flavorful addition to salads or used as potherbs. The seeds of the plant are also edible, and can be roasted to provide a crunchy texture and nutty taste. These are often used as a substitute for sunflower seeds in numerous dishes, or can simply be snacked on as they are.

MEDICINAL USE: Native American tribes used this plant for stomach problems, diuretics, febrifuge, and vulnerary properties. The root, leaves, and stems treat stomach pains, colds, fevers, and headaches.

HARVESTING: Leaves are best harvested when young. The roots can be harvested once the plant has matured. The seeds can be collected after the flowers have bloomed and dried.

CAUTION: Consumption of large quantities of leaves and petioles can induce sleepiness. Pregnant and breastfeeding women should consult a healthcare provider before using this plant medicinally.

across, with 4 rounded white petals, 6 yellowish stamens, a short central style, and a purplish-green ovary. Flowers are clustered at the tip of the stem.

FRUIT: Slender pod, up to 1 inch (0.25 cm) long, slightly curved, with a short beak at the tip.

SEED: Oval, reddish-brown when mature, arranged in 2 rows within the pod.

ROOT: Forms roots at the stem nodes when touching water or mud.

ODOR: Piquant, similar to mustard or radish.

EDIBLE USE: Watercress, one of the oldest known leafy vegetables consumed by humans, provides a zesty addition to salads, sandwiches, soups, sauces, and dips. It adds a peppery flavor to salads when combined with milder greens and plays a central role in the English watercress soup. It's also suitable for sautéing, stir-frying, or stewing. A popular alternative to the conventional basil pesto is watercress pesto, made by blending it with pine nuts, garlic, and Parmesan. The stems offer a crunchy texture in dishes, and its flowers can be used as a garnish or included in salads for a subtler flavor.

MEDICINAL USE: It can act as a disinfectant and healing agent, and all parts of the plant have strong antibiotic and antimicrobial properties. It provides a source of Vitamin C and may aid in combating bacteria, fungi, viruses, and even tumors.

HARVESTING: Optimal when the plant is young and tender. Avoid picking watercress when it becomes tough and bitter. Harvest by cutting stems above water, leaving some for regrowth, and avoid polluted or stagnant water areas. Rinse thoroughly post-harvest to remove any debris.

CAUTION: Watercress growing in polluted water can accumulate harmful bacteria or toxins.

General Information

OTHER NAMES: Yellowcress

HEIGHT: 1.6-4 feet (0.5-1.2 m) tall

HABITATS: Shallow streams, springs, ditches, ponds, and marshes

EDIBLE PARTS: Leaves, stems, seeds, flowers

30 Watercress
Nasturtium officinale

IDENTIFICATION FEATURES

STEM: Hollow, hairless, may be erect or sprawl across mud and water.

LEAF: Compound with 3 to 9 leaflets, shapes from lance-shaped to narrowly egg-shaped with uneven edges. Hairless and alternately arranged.

FLOWER: Small, about 1/4 inch (0.6 cm)

31 Tumble Mustard
Sisymbrium altissimum

IDENTIFICATION FEATURES

STEM: Slender, much-branched, hairy in the lower part, and hairless in the upper.

LEAF: Up to 8 inches (20 cm) long, deeply lobed. Lower leaves have rough, hairy edges and short stalked. Upper leaves are finely divided into linear segments, usually hairless.

FLOWER: Small, about 1/3 inch (0.85 cm) across, with 4 white to yellow petals and 6 stamens in the center. Flowers form in small clusters at the end of stems.

FRUIT: Thin pod, 2-4 inches (5-10 cm) long, with a brown tip.

SEED: Small, smooth, oval-shaped seeds ranging from dull orange to dark brown.

EDIBLE USE: The plant is edible and has a spicy flavor similar to wasabi or horseradish. The young leaves and shoots can be eaten raw or cooked as a salad or vegetable. The seeds, reminiscent of mustard, can be collected, dried, and ground into a powder. This powder is an excellent base for homemade mustard or can be used as a spice in various dishes.

General Information

OTHER NAMES: Tall hedge mustard

HEIGHT: Up to 5 feet (1.5 m) tall

HABITATS: Fields, roadsides, waste areas, and railroad tracks

EDIBLE PARTS: Young leaves, shoots, seeds

MEDICINAL USE: It has been used in traditional medicine for various ailments, such as coughs, asthma, bronchitis, sore throat, rheumatism, and kidney stones. The leaves can be chewed or made into tea or syrup for respiratory problems.

HARVESTING: Best when the plant is young and tender. The older leaves and stems become tough and bitter. To harvest the plant, cut off the stems near the base with a knife or scissors, and collect them in a basket or bag. Wash them well before eating or storing.

CAUTION: Generally considered safe to eat in moderate amounts, but some people may be allergic or sensitive to it. It may also interact with medications such as blood thinners or thyroid drugs.

General Information

OTHER NAMES: Wintercress, herb barbara, rocketcress

HEIGHT: 12 to 24 inches (30-60 cm) tall, with a maximum of 3 feet (90 cm)

HABITATS: Roadsides, fields, disturbed soil, river shores, meadows, wetlands, and forests

EDIBLE PARTS: Young leaves, shoots, flowers

32 Yellow Rocket
Barbarea vulgaris

IDENTIFICATION FEATURES

STEM: Stout, ribbed, and hairless, with colors ranging from light green to reddish-purple.

LEAF: Shiny, dark green leaves at the base, up to 6 inches (15 cm) long, with a large terminal lobe and smaller lower lobes. Smaller leaves higher up have fewer lobes. All leaves are hairless and shiny on top.

FLOWER: Clustered in dense terminals above foliage, each flower is 1/3 inches (0.85 cm) across with four bright yellow petals and four yellowish-green sepals.

FRUIT: Angular-cylindrical seedpod around 0.6-1.2 inches (1.5-3 cm) long, ascending along the racemes with a short slender beak at the end.

SEED: Ovoid, slightly flattened, brown in color, found within the seedpod.

EDIBLE USE: The leaves are edible when young and tender before they become bitter and hairy. They can be eaten raw or cooked as a salad green or a vegetable. They have a peppery flavor similar to arugula or watercress. They are rich in vitamin C, calcium, iron, and antioxidants. They can also be used as a substitute for mustard greens or horseradish in sauces and condiments. The flowers are also edible and can be added to salads or used as a garnish. They have a mild sweet flavor and a crunchy texture. They are also a good source of nectar for bees and butterflies.

MEDICINAL USE: Primarily supports the integumentary body system. It is commonly used as an astringent and is often used as a wound poultice.

HARVESTING: Best in spring or early summer, when the leaves are young, and tender and the flowers are just opening. Flowers bloom from April through June. The leaves and flowers can be picked by hand or cut with scissors or a knife.

CAUTION: Although generally safe, it can cause digestive upset if consumed in large quantities.

General Information

HEIGHT: 8-20 inches (20-50 cm) tall

HABITATS: Cultivated fields, gardens, road-sides, waste places, and disturbed soils

EDIBLE PARTS: Leaves, flowers, seeds

33 Shepherd's Purse
Capsella bursa-pastoris

IDENTIFICATION FEATURES

STEM: Grows 8-20 inches (20-50 cm) tall from a base of lobed leaves. The color varies from light green to dark reddish-purple, with a slightly hairy underside.

LEAF: Comes in two types. The base leaves start with smooth edges and develop lobes as they mature. The stem leaves are also lobed and grasp the stem.

FLOWER: Displays small white flowers with four petals in loose clusters. It can bloom at any time of the year.

FRUIT: A flat, heart-shaped pod, also known as a silicle, carrying multiple seeds.

SEED: Each pod contains about 20 shiny seeds, ranging from yellow to reddish-brown. They have a sticky substance that can trap small pests.

EDIBLE USE: The plant has a rich tradition of culinary use. Its peppery, cabbage-like flavor enhances salads when used raw, and its tender young leaves are a great addition to soups, stews, or stir-fries. The mature leaves have a more pronounced flavor and can be lightly boiled or steamed as a side dish. The flowers are also edible. The seeds can be used as a pepper substitute. Moreover, the plant is popular in traditional East Asian cuisine. It's often used in dumplings, rice cakes, or stir-fried with other vegetables, and it's a crucial ingredient in Korean soup.

MEDICINAL USE: It is used to stop bleeding and promote wound healing. It is also applied for burns, inflammation, and skin diseases.

HARVESTING: Ideally, pick the plant before flowering or early bloom. Hand-pick leaves and flowers, and collect mature seeds by shaking pods or rubbing them.

CAUTION: Consuming seeds and older leaves in large quantities can lead to digestive upset.

POISONOUS LOOK-ALIKES: *Thlaspi perfoliatum* (perfoliate penny-cress) is potentially toxic due to its concentration of heavy metals, particularly zinc.

• Seed Pods: *C. bursa-pastoris* has heart-shaped seed pods, while *T. perfoliatum* has round, flat seed pods.

• Leaves: The leaves of *T. perfoliatum* clasp around the stem (perfoliate), while *C. bursa-pastoris* leaves do not.

• Flowers: *T. perfoliatum* has white to light pink flowers.

Thlaspi perfoliatum

34 Hairy Bittercress
Cardamine hirsuta

IDENTIFICATION FEATURES

STEM: Slender, erect, smooth, or sparsely hairy.

LEAF: The plant has pinnately divided leaves. The leaves are bright green and pinnately divided with rounded or oval leaflets, with smooth or toothed edges. The basal leaves typically have several pairs of small leaflets and a larger terminal leaflet at the end. These leaves often form a rosette at the base of the plant. The stem leaves are alternate and smaller, generally with fewer leaflets.

FLOWER: The flowers are tiny, white, and consist of four petals. They grow in clusters at the top of the stem.

FRUIT: The fruits are slender, elongated seed pods called siliques that stand upright on the stem. The ripe fruit bursts when touched, dispersing the seeds far from the parent plant.

EDIBLE USE: The leaves and other tender parts

General Information
HEIGHT: 4-12 inches (10-30 cm) tall
HABITATS: Lawns, gardens, fields, and disturbed areas
EDIBLE PARTS: Leaves, flowers

of the plant are edible. The leaves can be consumed raw or cooked. Its peppery leaves can be used in salads, sandwiches, or garnish. They can also be lightly cooked and added to stir-fries, soups, or stews. The plant's tiny flowers can be used to add a bit of spice and visual appeal to salads or desserts.

MEDICINAL USE: Although not widely recognized for its medicinal properties, some people use hairy bittercress as a mild diuretic or to soothe coughs and sore throats.

HARVESTING: The best time to pick hairy bittercress is in the spring when the leaves are young and tender. To harvest, cut the plant at its base, leaving the roots in the ground.

General Information

OTHER NAMES: Least pepperwort

HEIGHT: 4-20 inches (10-50 cm) tall

HABITATS: Fields, gardens, roadsides, waste areas, disturbed sites

EDIBLE PARTS: Young leaves, seeds, and seed-pods

35 Virginia Pepperweed
Lepidium virginicum

IDENTIFICATION FEATURES

STEM: The stems are upright, branched, and covered with tiny hairs. They are light green to reddish-brown.

LEAF: The leaves are pinnately lobed in the basal rosette and become linear to lanceolate along the stem. The leaves are typically 2-4 inches (5-10 cm) long and have toothed margins.

FLOWER: The flowers are tiny, measuring less than 1/8 inch (about 3 mm) across, with four white petals and four green sepals. They appear in dense clusters atop slender stalks extending from the stem.

FRUIT: The fruits are round to oval-shaped pods known as silicles, up to 1/6 inch (0.4 cm) long. They are flat, notched at the top, and contain two seeds. The fruits are initially green, turning brown as they mature.

SEED: The seeds are small and reddish-brown. They are contained within the fruit and are typically dispersed when it splits open.

ODOR: The entire plant has a peppery taste, suggesting a strong, spicy odor.

EDIBLE USE: The young leaves, rich in protein, Vitamin A, and Vitamin C, can be consumed either raw or cooked. They add a spicy touch to salads with a hot cress-like flavor when chopped finely and used raw. Alternatively, they can be sautéed or used as a garnish. The young seedpods of the plant offer an interesting substitute for black pepper, introducing a pleasantly pungent flavor whether consumed raw or added as a condiment in soups and stews. The seeds can also be used as a substitute for pepper.

MEDICINAL USE: It has been traditionally used to treat digestive issues, respiratory problems, and skin conditions. It has also been used as a diuretic and stimulant.

HARVESTING: The best time to harvest virginia pepperweed is during the spring and early summer when the plant is young and tender. To harvest, simply cut the leaves, stems, and seedpods as needed.

CAUTION: Consuming in large quantities may cause stomach upset. It is best to use it in moderation.

POISONOUS LOOK-ALIKES: *Thlaspi perfoliatum* (perfoliate penny-cress). See descriptions on page 65.

36 Garlic Mustard
Alliaria petiolata

IDENTIFICATION FEATURES

STEM: The stem is erect, somewhat stout, and often hairless, appearing slightly purplish. It has a characteristic garlic-like odor when crushed.

LEAF: The leaves are alternate, kidney-shaped to heart-shaped, 4-6 inches (10-15 cm) long, with large teeth on the margin. They are dark green, with a somewhat wrinkled surface, and have a strong garlic smell when crushed.

FLOWER: The flowers are small, white, and borne in clusters at the top of the stem. Each flower has four petals arranged in a cross shape.

FRUIT: The fruit is a slender, four-sided, upright pod, called a silique, that is 1-2.5 inches (2.5-6.4 cm) long and contains small, black seeds. The pods start green and turn brown as they mature.

SEED: The seeds are small, black, oblong and contained within the fruit. When the fruit matures, it splits open to disperse the seeds.

General Information

OTHER NAMES: Hedge garlic

HEIGHT: 1-4 feet (0.3-1.2 m) tall

HABITATS: Disturbed areas, such as forest edges, roadsides, and along stream banks

EDIBLE PARTS: Young leaves, flowers, roots, and seeds

ROOT: The plant grows from a thin, deeply growing whitish taproot.

ODOR: When any part of the plant, especially the leaves or roots, is crushed or bruised, it releases a strong garlic smell. This helps in identifying the plant in the wild.

EDIBLE USE: This biennial plant is appreciated for its distinctive garlic and mustard flavor, a feature that makes it a versatile ingredient in many dishes. It's commonly used in salads and sauces, including pesto. While the young leaves are the most favored part due to their mild flavor, the flowers, roots, and seeds are also edible. The roots have a spicy flavor akin to horseradish, making them an interesting addition to various dishes. In autumn, the seeds can be collected and used as a seasoning.

MEDICINAL USE: It has been used traditionally for its antibacterial, antifungal, and diuretic properties. It has also been used to treat respiratory ailments like bronchitis and asthma.

HARVESTING: The best time to harvest garlic mustard is when the leaves are young and tender. The flowers can be picked in late spring and summer, while the seeds can be collected in the summer. To harvest, simply cut the leaves and stems as needed. The roots can be dug up in the fall.

CAUTION: Garlic mustard contains cyanide, which is toxic to many vertebrates. Proper preparation, such as chopping the plant, helps eliminate this risk.

37 American Hackberry
Celtis occidentalis

General Information

OTHER NAMES: Common hackberry, nettle-tree, sugarberry, beaverwood

HEIGHT: 30-50 feet (9-15 m) tall, with a maximum of 130 feet (40 m) in ideal conditions

HABITATS: Along rivers, streams, fence rows, roadsides and open woodlands

EDIBLE PARTS: Fruits

IDENTIFICATION FEATURES

BARK: Light brown or silvery gray, covered in corky warts or ridges. This pattern is more noticeable in younger trees.

STEM: Twigs transition in color from green to dark reddish gray. They are generally smooth, covered with small white lenticels, and have a zig-zag form.

LEAF: Bright green, rough on top, pale underneath, shaped like an egg or spear with a toothed margin from midleaf to tip.

FLOWER: Small, yellowish-green flowers that appear in April and May. The flowers include male, female, and "perfect" (having both male and female parts) flowers, all in the same plant.

FRUIT: Small, fleshy fruit that turns dark purple when ripe. It is less than an inch (2.5 cm) in length and width. Often remains on the tree in winter.

SEED: Each fruit holds one round, brown seed.

EDIBLE USE: The plant is notable for its edible fruits. These small, sweet, and nut-like fruits can be consumed raw. They can also be dried for later use, maintaining their sweetness and adding a pleasant chewy texture to baked goods like cookies, cakes, or muffins. The dried fruits can be finely ground into flour and used in bread or pancake recipes. Native American tribes traditionally used hackberry fruit to create a nutritious meal by grinding the dried fruits into fine powder.

MEDICINAL USE: The leaves can be used as a poultice for skin problems such as boils, ulcers, and wounds. The bark can be used as a tea for sore throat, coughs, colds, fever, diarrhea, dysentery, and urinary infections. The bark can also be chewed to relieve toothache.

HARVESTING: The best time to pick the fruits is when they are fully ripe and dark purple. The fruits can be harvested by shaking the branches or using a long fruit hook to collect them. The fruits should be washed and sorted before eating or processing.

CAUTION: It may cause mild stomach upset or allergic reactions in some people. The fruits may contain insect larvae or mold if not fresh or properly stored.

38 Chickweed
Stellaria media

IDENTIFICATION FEATURES

STEM: Succulent, green or burgundy, often displaying lines of white hair. Branches abundantly near the base, less so towards the tips.

LEAF: Green, hairless, oval to broadly elliptic. Up to 3/4 inch (1.9 cm) long and 1/2 inch (1.3 cm) wide. Larger and sit directly on the stem near stem tips; shorter petioles and slightly hairy near the base.

FLOWER: Small, 0.4 inch (1cm) in diameter, with 5 split white petals inside larger sepals that are often hairy. Each flower has 3-8 stamens and usually 3 styles.

FRUIT: Light brown, cylindrical seed capsule with 6 small teeth on the upper rim. Contains several seeds and forms year-round.

SEED: Reddish-brown, somewhat flat, and shaped like a kidney, with a slightly bumpy surface.

EDIBLE USE: Chickweed is a versatile edible plant that is high in vitamin C, iron, calcium, potassium, and other minerals. The tender leaves, stems, and flowers can be eaten raw in salads, where they add a fresh, crisp texture. Chickweed also works well as a cooked green, adding bulk and nutrition to soups, stir-fries, or it can be lightly steamed or sautéed on its own. Its delicate flavor pairs well with a bit of garlic and lemon. It can also be made into a pesto, combining chickweed with garlic, nuts, cheese, and olive oil for a unique spread that can be used on pasta, bread, or dip.

General Information

HEIGHT: Can reach up to 16 inches (41 cm) long, but usually stays closer to the ground

HABITATS: Lawns, gardens, fields, meadows, waste places, roadsides, and forest edges

EDIBLE PARTS: Leaves, flowers, stems, seeds

MEDICINAL USE: Traditionally used for diverse health issues, it possesses antiseptic, antifungal, antiviral, and antihistamine properties. It can be applied externally for skin conditions or taken internally for respiratory and digestive problems.

HARVESTING: Most abundant during the cooler months of spring. In milder climates, it can also be found throughout the winter. Flowers open in the morning for about 12 hours but not during dull weather. Leaves fold up at night. To harvest the plant, simply cut the stems and leaves and wash them well before using.

CAUTION: The leaves contain saponins. These compounds, though toxic, are poorly absorbed by the body and can be broken down by thorough cooking, reducing potential harm.

OTHER NAMES: Maidenstears

HEIGHT: 8-30 inches (20-76 cm) tall

HABITATS: Disturbed habitats such as roadsides, railroads, waste areas, and fields, but also grows in meadows, open woods, and shorelines

EDIBLE PARTS: Young leaves, shoots, stems

39 Bladder Campion
Silene vulgaris

IDENTIFICATION FEATURES

STEM: Light green and smooth, branching near its base.

LEAF: Up to 3 inches (7.6 cm) in length and 1.25 inches (3.2 cm) in width. It's shaped like a narrow lance, with no teeth on the edges and little to no hair. The leaf's tip is pointed, attaches directly to the stem without a stalk, and is rounded at the base where it attaches.

FLOWER: White with five petals, each one deeply split into two round lobes, about 1 inch (2.5 cm) long. Dark-tipped stamens and three styles extend out from the middle of the flower. The flower's base, or calyx, is light green to pinkish, with clear vein lines, and is usually puffed up like an oval balloon.

FRUIT: The fruit is a teardrop-shaped capsule containing small brown seeds enclosed by the calyx. When ripe, the capsule splits open along six teeth at the tip.

EDIBLE USE: *Silene vulgaris* is an edible plant primarily used in Mediterranean cuisine. The young leaves, shoots, and tips are often boiled and then sautéed with garlic and olive oil, used as a filling for pies or as an ingredient in risottos. The young stems, before flowering, can be pickled as a substitute for capers. In Spain, they are known as "collejas" and are used to make a dish called "gazpacho viudo", which consists of flatbread and a stew of Silene vulgaris leaves.

MEDICINAL USE: It has been used in traditional medicine for various ailments, such as coughs, colds, bronchitis, asthma, sore throat, urinary infections, wounds, and skin problems. It can be made into tea, syrup, a poultice, or an ointment.

HARVESTING: Best from spring to early fall when the plant is young and tender. Cut off the shoots and leaves with a knife or scissors, leaving some stems and roots intact so the plant can regrow. Wash the harvested parts thoroughly before using them.

CAUTION: Consuming large amounts of improperly prepared plants may lead to nausea, vomiting, or headaches due to potentially toxic compounds. It's advised to thoroughly cook it and avoid consumption during pregnancy, breastfeeding, or if taking certain medications.

40 Canadian Bunchberry

Cornus canadensis

IDENTIFICATION FEATURES

STEM: The stem is short, slender and often forms colonies from underground rhizomes.

LEAF: The leaves are oval to broadly elliptic, with a pointed tip. They are 1-2 inches (2.5-5 cm) long, glossy, dark green on top, and paler underneath. They are arranged oppositely, appearing in a whorl at the top of the stem, giving the plant a tiered look.

FLOWER: The true flowers are small and greenish-white, clustered in the middle of four large, white, or sometimes pink, petal-like bracts, which can be mistaken for petals. This arrangement creates an illusion of a single, large 1-2 inches (2.5-5 cm) flower. The flowers bloom in late spring to early fall.

FRUIT: The fruits are bright red, small (about 1/4 inch or 0.6 cm in diameter), and berry-like.

EDIBLE USE: The berries can be consumed raw or prepared in various ways. When eaten raw, they provide a delicate yet satisfying flavor. The berries' unique texture, which is somewhat dry and chewy, can be enhanced

General Information

OTHER NAMES: Canadian dwarf cornel, quatre-temps, crackerberry, creeping dogwood

HEIGHT: 4-8 inches (10–20 cm) tall

HABITATS: Cool, moist, shaded forests and woodland areas

EDIBLE PARTS: Fruits

through cooking. These berries can be pureed and combined with other fruits or integrated into desserts when cooked. They can be used in various culinary applications such as jams, jellies, sauces, syrups, and custards. They are also a suitable component for crafting steamed fruit puddings.

MEDICINAL USE: The leaves and stems have analgesic and febrifuge properties, traditionally used for treating aches, coughs, and fevers. The fruits act as anti-inflammatory, antispasmodic, and hypotensive.

HARVESTING: The fruits are harvested when they reach a ripe stage, typically in summer to early fall. The berries should be plump and a deep crimson color.

CAUTION: While generally safe, it's wise to test a small amount of new food for possible allergies.

41 American Persimmon

Diospyros virginiana

IDENTIFICATION FEATURES

BARK: The bark is dark gray or brown and divided into thick, almost square blocks. The older the tree gets, the deeper these fissures become.

LEAF: The leaves are simple and alternately arranged on the branches. They are oval to oblong with pointed tips, about 3-6 inches (7.6-15 cm) long, and half as wide. The upper surface is dark green and glossy, while the lower surface is lighter in color.

FLOWER: The tree has separate male and female flowers. Male flowers are small, yellowish, and occur in clusters, while female flowers are singular, larger, and creamy white.

FRUIT: The plant produces round or slightly oblong fruits about 1-2 inches (2.5-5 cm) in diameter. The fruits start green and turn bright to dark orange when ripe. They are sweet and have a custard-like consistency when fully ripe.

SEED: Each fruit contains up to 8 flat, oblong, and smooth seeds with a dark brown to black color.

EDIBLE USE: The fruits, when fully ripe, are sweet with a rich, honey-like flavor. They can be eaten fresh or used to make desserts such as persimmon puddings, cakes, and pies. The ripe fruit also lends itself well to preserves, jellies, and marmalades. In addition to sweet dishes, the persimmon can be used in savory recipes, pairing well with pork or poultry. Dried persimmon fruits make for a flavorful snack or can be used in trail mixes. Additionally, an oil from the seeds can be used that has a flavor akin to peanut oil. Leaves of the plant can be dried to make a tea rich in vitamin C. The roasted seed serves as a substitute for coffee.

MEDICINAL USE: The plant is used to treat bloody stools, scurvy (rich in Vitamin C), thrush, and sore throats and is used externally for warts or cancers.

HARVESTING: The fruit should be harvested when fully ripe. If unripe, it can be stored in a cool place to "blet." Bletting refers to the process of allowing the fruit to become very soft, almost to the point of rotting, which significantly enhances its flavors.

CAUTION: Consumption of unripe fruit should be avoided due to its highly astringent properties, which can cause mouth discomfort.

42 Large Cranberry
Vaccinium macrocarpon

IDENTIFICATION FEATURES

VINE/STEM: The plant produces slender, wiry stems from the vine that hold the fruit just above the surface.

LEAF: Evergreen, leathery, glossy, oblong to oval leaves that are 0.4-1 inch (1-2.5 cm) long with smooth or slightly toothed margins. Leaves are green above and pale green below, sometimes with a reddish tinge.

FLOWER: White or pink, bell-shaped, with four petals that are reflexed at the tips, exposing a tight cluster of stamens and a single long style. It is less than 1 inch (2.5 cm) in size.

FRUIT: Red or pink berries that are up to 1/2 inch (1.3 cm) across. The fruits mature in summer or fall and persist through winter.

EDIBLE USE: The plant is an essential ingredient in many North American dishes. The tart berries are often made into a sauce or jelly. They can also be used in baking, adding a tangy flavor to muffins, pies, and bread. Dried cranberries are a well-liked snack and can be added to salads, cereals, or trail mixes. Cranberries can be juiced and drunk or used in making cranberry wine or cocktails. Their

General Information

OTHER NAMES: Large cranberry, American cranberry

HEIGHT: 1-3 feet (0.3-0.9 m) tall

HABITATS: Bogs, marshes, swamps, wet meadows, and along streams and lakes

EDIBLE PARTS: Berries

flavor and high pectin content make them suitable for making fruit leathers and jams.

MEDICINAL USE: Traditionally used to manage urinary tract infections (UTIs) by hindering bacteria from attaching to bladder and urethra walls. They may also have potential anti-inflammatory, anti-cancer effects.

HARVESTING: The best time to harvest is from late summer to early fall, when the berries are ripe and deep red. To harvest them, one can use a rake or a scoop to gently pull them off the vines. The harvested berries should be washed and stored in a cool place or frozen for later use.

CAUTION: It can cause allergic reactions in some individuals, especially when consumed in large amounts. They're high in oxalates, potentially increasing kidney stone risk in susceptible individuals.

OTHER NAMES: Blue huckleberry, swamp blueberry

HEIGHT: 6-12 feet (1.8-3.7 m) tall

HABITATS: Moist woods, bogs, swamps, and low areas with acidic soils

EDIBLE PARTS: Berries, leaves

43 Highbush Blueberry
Vaccinium corymbosum

IDENTIFICATION FEATURES

BARK: Light brown or gray, it peels off and has thin furrows when the stems are old.

STEM: Yellow-green to reddish color in winter, with smooth and hairless new shoots.

LEAF: Dark glossy green, elliptical to ovate, up to 2 inches (5 cm) long with entire to serrate margins and pointed tips. They are arranged alternately on the stems and have prominent veins. When fall arrives, the leaves display a mix of red, yellow, orange, and purple.

FLOWER: White to light pink, bell-shaped, less than 1 inch (2.5 cm). Features five base-fused petals spreading out at the mouth, ten stamens, and a central protruding pistil. Borne in clusters at branch ends.

FRUIT: Small, round berries that are less than 1 inch (2.5 cm) in diameter, blue to purple when ripe.

EDIBLE USE: The berries are edible and nutritious, rich in antioxidants, vitamin C, fiber, and manganese. Eaten fresh, they are a delicious and nutritious snack. The berries can be used in a wide range of culinary applications, from baking - where they shine in muffins, pies, and pancakes - to making sauces, jams, and jellies. They also freeze well, allowing for their use long after the harvest season has passed. Blueberry wine is a popular home-made ferment, and the juice can be used in smoothies or cocktails. Dried blueberries can be used similarly to raisins in granolas, cookies or as a topping for yogurt or cereals. The leaves are used for making herbal tea.

MEDICINAL USE: Native Americans used leaves and roots to treat conditions like coughs, diarrhea, kidney stones, and wounds.

HARVESTING: The best time to pick the berries is when they are fully ripe. The berries should be firm, plump, and blue all over, with no green or red spots. They should also detach easily from the stem when gently pulled. Avoid picking berries that are wet or moldy. Refrigerate or freeze the berries as soon as possible after picking them to preserve their quality.

CAUTION: It's important not to consume the leaves in large quantities, as they contain small amounts of a toxic compound.

44 Bog Blueberry
Vaccinium uliginosum

IDENTIFICATION FEATURES

BARK: Dark brown or copper, thin and smooth, peels off easily.

STEM: Slender, red on new growth, aging to reddish-brown or brown; older ones turn smooth gray.

LEAF: Simple, alternate, oval, or elliptic, smooth or slightly toothed edges. The leaves are dark green above and paler below, with a distinctive net-like pattern of veins.

FLOWER: Four-parted, urn-shaped flowers that stay closed in bud. The flowers are white or pinkish-white and are borne in clusters of two to six at the ends of the branches.

FRUIT: Round or oval berries that are blue-black or purple-black when ripe. The berries are 0.2-0.35 inch (5-9 mm) in diameter, with a thin skin and a juicy pulp.

EDIBLE USE: Bog blueberry is a northern species cherished for its berries. They have a slightly tart yet sweet flavor, perfect for fresh eating. They are fantastic in baked goods, from muffins and pancakes to pies and tarts. They can be turned into jams, jellies, or sauces, which pair well with sweet and savory

General Information

OTHER NAMES: Bog bilberry, tundra bilberry

HEIGHT: 4–30 inches (10-76 cm) tall

HABITATS: Mountain summits and plateaus, bogs, and open coniferous forests

EDIBLE PARTS: Berries, leaves

dishes. The berries can be dried for long-term storage, used in trail mixes, granolas, or rehydrated for baked goods. Additionally, they can be used to make a vibrant blueberry wine or added to smoothies for a nutritious boost. Fresh or dried leaves are often used for herbal tea.

MEDICINAL USE: Berries and leaves are used for enhancing blood circulation, lowering blood pressure, preventing scurvy, reducing inflammation, healing wounds, soothing sore throats, relieving diarrhea, and boosting the immune system.

HARVESTING: The best time to harvest berries is from late summer to early fall when they are ripe and have a dark blue color. The berries can be easily detached from the stems by hand or with a berry picker.

CAUTION: It's important not to consume the leaves in large quantities, as they contain small amounts of a toxic compound.

45 Wintergreen
Gaultheria procumbens

IDENTIFICATION FEATURES

STEM: Not aromatic; characterized by its creeping stems.

LEAF: Dark green, elliptical or ovate, and about 1-2 inches (2.5-5 cm) long; shiny appearance on the upper surface while lighter green on the underside; have a distinctive wintergreen scent and taste.

FLOWER: Small, white or pale pink, and bell-shaped; they hang from the tips of the stems in small clusters.

FRUIT: Bright red berries, about 0.4 inches (1 cm) in diameter.

ODOR: Known for the strong wintergreen scent that is released when the leaves are crushed.

EDIBLE USE: Wintergreen is renowned for its refreshingly minty, sweet berries, which can be eaten raw, made into a unique jelly, or used as a natural flavoring in candies and desserts. The leaves, known for their strong wintergreen scent, can be used fresh or dried to make a flavorful tea. They can also be infused in water to make a refreshing minty drink, or in milk to create a dessert sauce. The plant's essential oil is used as a flavoring in candies, chewing gum, toothpaste, and mouthwash.

MEDICINAL USE: It has traditionally been used as a pain reliever, particularly for joint and muscle pain. It also has antispasmodic and anti-inflammatory properties. The essential oil from the plant is used in topical analgesic preparations.

HARVESTING: Wintergreen leaves can be harvested any time of year. The berries can be picked when they are ripe and bright red. Be sure to harvest responsibly and avoid over-harvesting, as wintergreen is a slow-growing plant.

CAUTION: Wintergreen oil can be toxic when ingested in large quantities, so it's important to use it sparingly and with caution. Pregnant and breastfeeding women, as well as people with liver or kidney issues, should consult a healthcare professional before using wintergreen medicinally.

OTHER NAMES: Potato bean, hopniss, Indian potato, cinnamon vine

HEIGHT: The vine can grow to 3-20 feet (0.9-6 m) long

HABITATS: Riverbanks, wetlands, forests, and thickets

EDIBLE PARTS: Tubers, seeds and seed pods

46 Groundnut
Apios americana

IDENTIFICATION FEATURES

STEM: Twining, green in color, and can sometimes be hairy.

LEAF: Pinnate with 5-7 leaflets that are teardrop-shaped and bright green. They are 3-6 inches (7.6-15 cm) long and have smooth edges. The leaflets are arranged alternately along the main stem.

FLOWER: Pea-like and borne in dense racemes that are 3-5 inches (7.6-12.7 cm) long. They are pale brown outside and dark reddish-brown inside and have a sweet scent. They have five petals and bloom from mid-summer to fall in the leaf axils.

FRUIT: Legumes (pods) that are 2-5 inches (5-12.7 cm) long and bean-shaped. They are green when immature and brown when mature. They contain several seeds that are oval and brownish-black.

TUBER: Edible and large, they are rhizomatous stems, not roots.

EDIBLE USE: The most edible part of Groundnut is the tuber, which has brown skin and white flesh that is starchy and nutty in flavor. They can be boiled, roasted, or fried and have a nutty, slightly sweet flavor that complements a wide range of dishes. They can be used in stews, soups, or mashed as a side dish. The tubers can be dried and ground into flour, used in making bread or thickening sauces. The young pods and seeds can be cooked and eaten.

MEDICINAL USE: Used by Native Americans in treating kidney stones, urinary infections, rheumatism, diabetes, and snake bites. The tubers are also said to have aphrodisiac properties and increase fertility.

HARVESTING: The best time to harvest the tubers is in late fall or winter when the vines die back, and the tubers are fully mature. The tubers can be dug up with a shovel or a fork, but they are often deep and hard to find. The tubers can be kept in a cool and dry place for several months. The seeds can be harvested when they are green and tender.

CAUTION: Always cook tubers before eating, as they can be toxic when eaten raw. Some people may have allergic reactions to it, especially if they are allergic to peanuts or other legumes.

General Information

OTHER NAMES: Lucerne

HEIGHT: Up to 3.3 feet (1 m) tall

HABITATS: Roadsides, waste areas, disturbed sites, dry fields

EDIBLE PARTS: Sprouts, leaves, shoots

47 Alfalfa
Medicago sativa

IDENTIFICATION FEATURES

STEM: Much branched, hairless to sparsely hairy.

LEAF: Compound leaves with three leaflets, up to 1 inch (2.5 cm) long. Leaflets have small teeth at the tip and a prominent midrib. Usually green or gray-green. Attached to a long petiole connected to the stem at a node. Leaves are arranged alternately along the stem.

FLOWER: Small, pea-shaped, and purple, in round or short cylindrical clusters. Each flower is up to 1/3 inch (0.85 cm) long. Five petals: one large upper petal, two lateral petals, and two lower petals.

FRUIT: Coiled pods with 10 to 20 seeds. Green when young, turning brown when mature. Twisted with spines or hairs on the surface. Split open when dry.

SEED: Yellow-brown, kidney-shaped seeds within the pods. Approximately 0.08-0.12 inches (2-3 mm) long.

EDIBLE USE: The plant provides high-quality protein, fiber, vitamins, minerals, and antioxidants. It can be consumed in various forms, such as alfalfa sprouts, alfalfa tea, alfalfa juice, alfalfa tablets, or alfalfa powder. Alfalfa sprouts are commonly added to salads, sandwiches, soups, or stir-fries for their crunchy texture and mild flavor. Alfalfa tea is made by steeping dried alfalfa leaves in boiling water for 10 to 15 minutes. Alfalfa juice is extracted from fresh alfalfa leaves using a juicer or blender. Alfalfa tablets or powders are dietary supplements that contain concentrated alfalfa extracts or dried alfalfa leaves.

MEDICINAL USE: It is used for various conditions such as digestive issues, kidney stones, and high cholesterol. It has potential anti-inflammatory and antioxidant properties, but more research is needed.

HARVESTING: Use scissors or garden shears to snip off the young leaves and tender stems. It's best to harvest in the morning when the plant is most hydrated. Tie them into compact bundles and hang them upside down in an airy place until completely dry.

CAUTION: Those allergic to legumes or related plants should avoid alfalfa. It's not recommended for people with certain autoimmune diseases, hormone-sensitive cancers, or those taking specific medications like warfarin or thyroid hormones without consulting a doctor.

OTHER NAMES: Yellow melilot, ribbed melilot, common melilot

HEIGHT: Up to 4-6 feet (1.2-1.8 m) tall at maturity

HABITATS: Open disturbed land, prairies, roadsides, fields, pastures, and waste places

EDIBLE PARTS: Young leaves, shoots, seed pods, flowers

48 Yellow Sweet Clover
Melilotus officinalis

IDENTIFICATION FEATURES

STEM: Grooved with minimal hairs, colored either green or tinged with red.

LEAF: The leaves are green and have three leaflets each. The leaflets are oval-shaped with toothed margins. The leaflets are about 0.5-1 inch (1.3-2.5 cm) long and 0.2-0.4 inch (0.5-1 cm) wide.

FLOWER: The flowers are yellow and arranged in long spikes at the end of the branches. The flowers are small and have five petals each. The flowers have a sweet odor and bloom from May to September.

FRUIT: The fruits are small pods that contain one seed each. The pods are wrinkled and about 0.1-0.2 inch (0.25-0.5 cm) long.

ODOR: The plant has a characteristic sweet odor.

EDIBLE USE: The plant can be used as pasture or livestock feed. It can also be eaten by humans as cooked vegetable when young and tender, but it may have a bitter taste due to the presence of coumarin in the plant. Its leaves are often used as a flavoring herb in cooking. They impart a sweet, vanilla-like flavor that complements various dishes, such as soups, stews, and salads. The flowers are edible and can add color and a touch of sweetness to salads or as a garnish.

MEDICINAL USE: It has been used to treat varicose veins, insomnia, nervous tension, flatulence, and more. It can also be used topically for eye inflammations, rheumatic pains, and other skin conditions.

HARVESTING: The best time to pick the plant is when it is young and tender or in full bloom. To harvest the plant, use scissors or garden shears to snip the plant parts you want.

CAUTION: The plant contains coumarin, which can act as a blood thinner when improperly dried or fermented. Only consume fresh plants, avoid large amounts, and consult a doctor if you have clotting issues or are taking blood thinners.

OTHER NAMES: Dutch clover

HEIGHT: 3-6 inches (5-15 cm) tall

HABITATS: Lawns, meadows, pastures, and other open, well-drained areas

EDIBLE PARTS: Stems, leaves, flowers, and seed pods

49 White Clover
Trifolium repens

IDENTIFICATION FEATURES

STEM: The plant spreads through stolons, which are horizontal stems that root at the nodes.

LEAF: The leaves are compound, trifoliate (having three leaflets), and measure about 1/2 inch (1.3 cm) in diameter. Each leaflet is oval or elliptical in shape, with a characteristic pale V-shaped mark on the upper surface. The leaf margins are smooth or slightly serrated, and the base of the leafstalk often has two small, lance-shaped stipules.

FLOWER: White clover has small, white, or pale pink flowers arranged in dense, spherical, or oval clusters (inflorescences) that measure 1/2 to 1 inch (1.3-2.5 cm) in diameter. Each flower is tubular and measures about 1/8 inch (3 mm) long.

FRUIT: The fruits are small, brown seed pods that are hidden within the flower head. Each pod contains 3 to 6 tiny seeds.

SEED: Each pod contains 3 to 6 tiny seeds.

ODOR: The stem is aromatic.

EDIBLE USE: The edible parts are the stems, leaves, flowers, and seed pods. The leaves can be eaten raw or cooked as leafy greens or dried to add a vanilla flavor to baked goods. The flowers, when fresh, can serve as a decorative garnish or dried to make herbal tea, jelly, or flour. The seed pods can be dried and ground into flour or roasted and eaten as a snack. The stems can be cooked like asparagus.

MEDICINAL USE: Traditionally, white clover has been used to treat various ailments, including coughs, colds, and skin irritations. It is also known for its blood-purifying properties and has been used to treat gout and rheumatism.

HARVESTING: Flowers can be collected throughout the blooming season, typically lasting from spring to late summer. Leaves are edible and can be harvested when needed. To harvest, simply pick the leaves and flowers by hand or use scissors to cut them close to the base.

CAUTION: White clover is generally considered safe to eat but may cause gastrointestinal discomfort in some individuals, particularly when consumed in large quantities.

50 Hog-peanut
Amphicarpaea bracteata

General Information

OTHER NAMES: Ground bean

HEIGHT: Varies based on support structure (twines around other plants)

HABITATS: Woodlands, thickets, and moist slopes

EDIBLE PARTS: Seeds, Roots

IDENTIFICATION FEATURES

STEM: Thin and twining, often climbing over other plants, and it's hairy.

LEAVES: The leaves are trifoliate, meaning each leaf has three leaflets. The leaflets are elliptic or egg-shaped and have pointed tips. They are arranged alternately along the stem.

FLOWERS: The plant produces two types of flowers. The more noticeable ones are the small, pink to lavender, butterfly-like flowers that are formed in clusters on slender, upright stalks. They are typically about 0.2 inch (0.5 cm) long and consist of 5 petals with the typical "banner, wings, and keel" arrangement common in the pea family. The second type is inconspicuous flowers near the plant base, which self-fertilize and create underground pods.

FRUITS: This plant produces two types of fruits. The aerial fruits are pods that are about 2-3 inches (5-7.6 cm) long and contain several seeds. They are initially green, turning brown as they mature. The underground fruits are also pods.

SEEDS: The plant produces two types of seeds, those from aerial fruits and those from underground fruits. The seeds from the aerial fruits are small and dark, while those from the underground fruits are larger.

ROOTS: The plant has a system of rhizomes and tuberous roots. The tubers are small, rounded, and edible.

EDIBLE USE: The plant offers various edible parts, including seeds and roots. The lower seeds are in pods that submerge just below the soil level. They can be used as a substitute for peanuts. The upper part of the plant yields smaller seeds housed in pods that stay above ground. These seeds, high in protein, are typically cooked before eating. Furthermore, the roots, although sometimes small and stringy, can be peeled, boiled, and eaten.

MEDICINAL USE: The root has been used to treat diarrhea and snake bites, while pulverized leaves are applied to swellings.

HARVESTING: The larger seeds can be harvested throughout winter. These are found in pods just below the soil's surface. The smaller seeds from flowers higher up the plant can also be collected, though they are less abundant and more challenging to harvest. The roots can be harvested, but they often turn out to be small and stringy.

OTHER NAMES: Red beech, ridge beech

HEIGHT: 52-115 feet (16 to 35 m) tall, and sometimes up to 120 feet (37 m) in favorable conditions

HABITATS: Mixed hardwood forests

EDIBLE PARTS: Nuts, young leaves, inner bark

51 American Beech
Fagus grandifolia

IDENTIFICATION FEATURES

BARK: Thin, smooth, and light gray. Remains smooth as the tree ages.

LEAF: Leaves are dark green, oval to elliptic, with coarse teeth along the margins and parallel veins that end at the tips of the teeth. Leaves are 2.4-4.7 inches (6-12 cm) long and 1.2-2.8 inches (3-7 cm) wide.

FLOWER: Small, yellowish-green flowers. The male flowers are arranged in drooping, globular clusters that hang from the twigs. The female flowers are borne in short spikes that arise from the leaf axils or near the ends of the branches.

FRUIT: Fruits are nuts enclosed by spiny bracts that form a four-lobed husk. The nuts are triangular, brown, shiny, and about 0.6 inch (1.5 cm) long.

EDIBLE USE: The nuts have a sweet, slightly astringent taste and can be enjoyed raw or cooked. They can be roasted or boiled to remove their bitter tannins and make them more palatable. They can also be ground into flour or used as a substitute for coffee beans. The young, tender, and slightly sweet leaves can be cooked and eaten. The inner bark can be dried, pulverized into flour, and used as an emergency food source for bread-making.

MEDICINAL USE: The bark is an astringent, antiseptic, and tonic, while the leaves can be used for inflammation, and the nuts can expel intestinal worms.

HARVESTING: The nuts should be collected when fully mature. The inner shells should be removed by hand. The nuts should be dried or roasted and stored in a cool and dry place.

CAUTION: Consuming large amounts of the raw seeds can be toxic due to the presence of tannins. Those with nut allergies or kidney problems are advised to avoid them.

POISONOUS LOOK-ALIKES: *Aesculus glabra* (Ohio buckeye) .

• Leaves: *F. grandifolia* has simple, alternate leaves with a pointed tip, while *A. glabra* has palmately compound leaves.

• Fruit: *A. glabra* produces a toxic, spiny husked fruit.

Aesculus glabra

52 White Oak
Quercus alba

IDENTIFICATION FEATURES

BARK: Whitish or light gray with deep, irregular furrows and flattened ridges. The bark tends to form overlapping scales halfway up the trunk, providing a distinct identifying feature.

LEAF: 4-9 inches (10-23 cm) long and 2-4 inches (5-10 cm) wide, fingerlike lobed leaves with 5-9 deep rounded lobes; bright green color on top and paler green underneath, turning to a deep red or brown in the fall.

FLOWER: Small, greenish-yellow flowers in catkins that appear in spring; male catkins are slender and drooping, while female flowers are tiny and appear in short spikes.

FRUIT: An acorn, approximately 0.6-1 inch (1.5-2.5 cm) long, with a warty, bowl-shaped cap that covers about a quarter of the nut; acorns are light brown and typically mature in one season.

EDIBLE USE: White oak provides acorns, a significant food source for indigenous cultures. These acorns, known for their less bitter taste compared to other oak species, can be ground into nutritious flour. This acorn flour can be used in breads, pancakes, or other baked goods. The acorns can also be roasted and used as a coffee substitute. Before consuming, the acorns should be leached off their tannins by soaking them in water for several hours, then draining and repeating the process until the water runs clear.

General Information

HEIGHT: 80-100 feet (24 to 30 m) tall

HABITATS: Found in a variety of habitats, such as upland woods, slopes, and well-drained lowlands

EDIBLE PARTS: Acorns

MEDICINAL USE: The inner bark can be made into a tea to treat diarrhea, dysentery, and hemorrhoids. A poultice of the leaves can be applied topically to heal wounds, burns, and skin irritations.

HARVESTING: The best time to harvest white oak acorns is in late summer or fall when they fall from the tree. Collect acorns free of blemishes, insect damage, or mold, and discard any with small holes, which may indicate the presence of insects.

CAUTION: White oak acorns can be eaten but need proper processing to remove tannins that can cause stomach and kidney issues. Also, some people might be allergic to acorns or other parts of the tree.

53 Black Walnut
Juglans nigra

IDENTIFICATION FEATURES

BARK: Dark gray to black, with deep, furrowed ridges.

LEAF: Pinnately compound leaves with 15-23 leaflets, which are dark green, smooth, and have an alternate arrangement on the stem. The leaflets have serrated edges and are somewhat lance-shaped.

FLOWER: Small, greenish-yellow flowers that appear in drooping catkins that are 3-5 inches (7.6-12.7 cm) long. The plant has male and female flowers on the same tree, but they are separate.

FRUIT: Large, round, and green, measuring 2-2.5 inches (5-6.4 cm) in diameter. They have a thick, green, and somewhat fleshy husk surrounding the hard, dark brown, deeply grooved nut.

SEED: The nut contains a rich, flavorful, and highly prized kernel.

EDIBLE USE: The plant provides a rich, distinctive nut that is prized in culinary applications. The nuts have a robust, nutty flavor that is more intense than the common English walnut. They can be enjoyed raw or toasted, and add a delightful crunch and flavor to salads, pastries, and meat dishes. Black wal-

General Information

HEIGHT: Up to 130 feet (39 m) tall

HABITATS: Hardwood and mixed forest, savannas, banks

EDIBLE PARTS: Nuts, sap

nuts are also excellent in baked goods, like cookies and brownies, and can be used to make a flavorful oil. In spring, the tree's sweet sap, similar to sugar maple's, can be tapped and transformed into syrup or sugar.

MEDICINAL USE: The plant has antifungal, antimicrobial, and anti-parasitic properties. The green hulls can be used to treat skin conditions like ringworm and athlete's foot.

HARVESTING: The best time to harvest black walnuts is in summer and fall, when the nuts begin to fall from the tree. Collect the nuts and remove the outer green husk. Once the husk is removed, allow the nuts to dry in a well-ventilated area for several weeks. After drying, you can crack the hard shells to extract the nutmeat.

CAUTION: Some people may be allergic to black walnuts. The green husks contain a chemical called juglone, which can be toxic in large amounts and cause skin irritation. Always handle with gloves.

54 Shagbark Hickory
Carya ovata

IDENTIFICATION FEATURES

BARK: Dark brown, peeling bark that forms long, loose, curling strips on mature trees.

BRANCH: Strong and spread out, making a rounded crown. Twigs are stout, with brown color and light lenticels.

LEAF: Compound leaves consisting of 5-7 broadly lance-shaped leaflets with finely serrated margins, about 3-7 inches (7.6-17.8 cm) long and 1-3 inches (2.5-7.6 cm) wide, arranged alternately on the stem; the terminal leaflet is the largest.

FLOWER: The tree is monoecious, with separate male (yellow-green catkins) and female (small and clustered) flowers.

FRUIT: A large, round nut enclosed in a thick, hard husk; the husk starts green and turns brown as it matures, splitting open to release a light brown nut with a thin shell

EDIBLE USE: The nuts are the primary edible part of the tree. After removing the husk and cracking the shell, the nutmeat can be eaten raw, roasted, or used as an ingredient

General Information

HEIGHT: 60-100 feet (18-30 m) tall

HABITATS: Hardwood forest, upland slopes

EDIBLE PARTS: Nut, bark

in various dishes. The nuts have a sweet, rich flavor and are commonly used in baking or as a topping for salads, oatmeal, and other dishes. They can be ground into flour or used in baked goods or processed into nut milk. The hickory nuts can also be used to make syrup. Additionally, the bark can be used to flavor a syrup reminiscent of maple syrup.

MEDICINAL USE: The bark is traditionally used for minor skin issues, and the nut oil is sometimes used for rheumatic conditions.

HARVESTING: The best time to harvest the nuts is in summer and fall. Once you have gathered the nuts, remove the husks, and let them dry for a few days before cracking the shells and extracting the nutmeat.

CAUTION: The nuts are generally safe to eat but can be a potential allergen for some individuals. If you have a known tree nut allergy, avoiding consuming the nuts.

55 Creeping Charlie
Glechoma hederacea

IDENTIFICATION FEATURES

STEM: Square, hairy, and often reddish-green stems that root at the nodes where they touch the ground.

LEAF: Round to kidney-shaped, with round-toothed edges and prominent veins. They are opposite on the stem and have long petioles that attach to the leaf's center. The leaves are about 0.8-1.2 inches (2-3 cm) in diameter and have a hairy upper surface. They are aromatic when crushed and have a minty smell.

FLOWER: Symmetrical and funnel-shaped, blue or purple. Grown in pairs or trios at the base of leaves. Each flower features a single pistil with a split style and four stamens - two long and two short.

FRUIT: Oval pods, containing 4 dark brown, ovoid nutlets.

ODOR: The leaves are aromatic when crushed and have a minty smell.

EDIBLE USE: The young leaves can be eaten raw or cooked. They have a minty flavor and can be used as a salad green, a garnish, or a flavoring agent. They can also be brewed into a tea that has a pleasant aroma and taste. The tea is said to have diuretic, expectorant, and anti-inflammatory properties. Some people also use the leaves to make soups and other dishes.

MEDICINAL USE: This plant is rich in potassium and iron and may reduce inflammation and cleanse the lungs, kidneys, stomach, and bowels.

HARVESTING: The best time to pick the leaves is when they are young and tender. It is advisable to wash the plant thoroughly before using it, as it may have dirt or pesticides on it.

CAUTION: Excessive consumption may lead to digestive problems or allergic reactions. It should be avoided by pregnant or breastfeeding individuals as it may affect hormones.

56 Bee Balm
Monarda fistulosa

IDENTIFICATION FEATURES

STEM: Bee balm has square, hollow stems, with few erect branches.

LEAF: The leaves are opposite, lance-shaped, and toothed along the edges. They measure 2-4 inches (5-10 cm) long and have a minty fragrance when crushed.

FLOWER: Bee balm has tubular, lavender to pinkish-purple flowers arranged in dense, terminal clusters. Each flower is two-lipped, with the upper lip forming a hood and the lower lip spreading into three lobes.

FRUIT: The fruits are small, brown, oval-shaped nutlets that develop within the calyx after the flowers fade.

ODOR: The plant has a distinct, minty aroma.

EDIBLE USE: The plant is often used as a flavoring in various dishes. The leaves can be used fresh or dried, adding a unique, minty flavor to salads, soups, stews, and sauces. The crushed leaves can be used as a seasoning for meat, poultry, and fish. The leaves can also be used to make a flavorful tea. The flowers,

General Information

OTHER NAMES: Wild bergamot

HEIGHT: Up to 3 feet (0.9 m) tall

HABITATS: Meadows, prairies, open woodlands, and along roadsides

EDIBLE PARTS: Leaves, stems, flowers

being visually appealing, can be used in salads or garnish, adding a touch of color and a mild, minty flavor.

MEDICINAL USE: The plant has been used traditionally for various medicinal purposes, including treating respiratory ailments, digestive issues, and skin conditions.

HARVESTING: The best time to harvest Bee Balm leaves is from early summer, just before the plant begins to flower. The flowers can be harvested as they open throughout the summer. To harvest, simply pick the leaves and flowers by hand or use scissors to cut them close to the stem.

CAUTION: Bee balm is generally considered safe to eat, but some individuals may experience skin irritation or allergic reactions when handling the plant.

57 Self-heal
Prunella vulgaris

IDENTIFICATION FEATURES

STEM: Self-heal has a creeping, square-shaped stem often tinged with purple.

LEAF: The leaves are simple, egg-shaped to lance-shaped, and measure 1-2 inches (2.5-5 cm) long. They are dark green and have serrated edges. The leaves are arranged oppositely along the stem.

FLOWER: Self-heal flowers are tubular, purple to pink, and grow in dense, cylindrical spikes at the top of the stem. Each flower has a distinctive "hooded" appearance, with the upper lip forming a protective hood over the lower lip. The flowering period typically occurs from May to September.

FRUIT: The fruits of self-heal are small, inconspicuous, and consist of tiny, dark brown to black seeds contained within the dried flower calyx.

SEED: The seeds of self-heal are tiny, dark brown to black.

EDIBLE USE: Self-heal is a versatile culinary herb. The leaves can be incorporated raw into salads or used in cooked dishes such as

General Information
OTHER NAMES: Heart-of-the-earth, carpenter's herb
HEIGHT: 2-12 inches (5-30 cm) tall
HABITATS: Meadows, fields, lawns, woodland edges, and roadsides
EDIBLE PARTS: Leaves

soups, stews, and stir-fries. Despite a slight bitterness due to the tannin presence, a simple wash can reduce this. The plant also makes a refreshing herbal tea, offering a pleasant taste and health benefits. Drying the leaves allows for long-term storage and year-round culinary use.

MEDICINAL USE: It has a long history of use in traditional medicine for various ailments. It has been used to treat sore throats, inflammation, wounds, and digestive issues. The plant is thought to have antibacterial, anti-inflammatory, and antioxidant properties.

HARVESTING: The best time to harvest self-heal is when the leaves are young and tender. To harvest, simply snip off the leaves with scissors or a knife.

OTHER NAMES: Blue giant hyssop, fragrant giant hysso

HEIGHT: 2-4 feet (0.6-1.2 m) tall

HABITATS: Prairies, meadows, and open woodlands

EDIBLE PARTS: Leaves, flowers

58 Anise Hyssop
Agastache foeniculum

IDENTIFICATION FEATURES

STEM: The stems are square, green, and straight. They are aromatic and contribute to the plant's licorice or anise scent.

LEAF: Broad lance-shaped, 2-4 inches (5-10 cm) long, with serrated edges; green on the upper surface and slightly lighter on the underside. They bear a fragrant aroma.

FLOWER: Small, tubular, and lavender-blue, densely arranged in a spike at the top of the stem, with each flower measuring about 1.3 inches (3.3 cm); bloom from summer to fall.

FRUIT: The fruits are very small, dry, brown, and do not split open when mature.

SEED: The seeds inside the fruit are tiny and brown.

ODOR: Leaves and stems have a distinctive anise or licorice scent.

EDIBLE USE: The plant has a strong licorice flavor and is often used as a seasoning. The leaves and flowers can be consumed fresh or dried in salads, soups, desserts, and flavor beverages, from water to cocktails. The flowers are a visually appealing garnish for salads and desserts. A delicious herbal tea can be made from leaves and flowers, either fresh or dried. It can also be used to flavor honey or sugar. The plant is also a favorite for making liqueurs and other beverages.

MEDICINAL USE: It has been used traditionally to treat colds, coughs, and digestive issues. It is also believed to have mild sedative and anti-inflammatory properties.

HARVESTING: The leaves, known for their fragrant aroma and flavor, can be harvested throughout their growing period, usually when fully grown and robust. Flowers, which are also edible, are typically collected from June through late fall during their full bloom.

CAUTION: While the plant is generally considered safe, people with allergies to plants in the mint family (Lamiaceae) should exercise caution. Women who are pregnant or breastfeeding are advised to consult a healthcare professional before consuming the plant.

General Information

OTHER NAMES: White sassafras, red sassafras, silky sassafras

HEIGHT: 50-66 feet (15–20 m) tall

HABITATS: Open woods, roadsides, and disturbed areas

EDIBLE PARTS: Leaves, young shoots, roots, root bark

59 Sassafras
Sassafras albidum

IDENTIFICATION FEATURES

BARK: The bark on the trunk of mature trees is thick, dark red-brown, and deeply furrowed.

LEAF: Medium green, 4 to 6 inches (10-15 cm) long, 2 to 4 inches (5-10 cm) wide, alternate arrangement, with entire to lobed margins. The leaves present three main shapes: unlobed and ovate, mitten-shaped, and three-lobed, all of which can be found on the same branch. The leaf color transitions from a bright green on the upper surface to paler or white beneath, with a fall color of yellow, tinged with red.

FLOWER: Yellow to greenish-yellow, with five or six tepals and no petals but six greenish-yellow sepals. Produced in loose, drooping, few-flowered racemes up to 2 inches (5 cm) long.

FRUIT: Dark blue-black drupes, about 0.4 inch (1 cm) long, each containing a single seed and borne on a red fleshy, club-shaped pedicel. These fruits are produced in pendant clusters on female trees, held in red, cup-like receptacles on red stalks.

SEED: Contained within the dark blue-black drupe, thick and fleshy cotyledons.

ROOT: The roots are thick and fleshy and frequently produce root sprouts which can develop into new trees.

ODOR: All parts of the plant are aromatic and spicy.

EDIBLE USE: The roots and root bark of sassafras were traditionally used to make root beer, and the plant gives the beverage its distinctive flavor. The root bark is also used as a tea, known as sassafras tea, with a somewhat sweet flavor. Sassafras leaves can be dried and ground into a powder known as filé powder, which is used as a thickening agent and flavoring in Cajun and Creole cooking, particularly in gumbo. Young shoots and leaves are sometimes used in salads and soups.

MEDICINAL USE: It is used to treat gastrointestinal complaints, colds, kidney ailments, rheumatism, and skin eruptions.

HARVESTING: It's best to harvest Sassafras's leaves when they're fully developed yet tender. Collect young shoots in the spring when they're most tender. For roots, which contain the highest aromatic compounds, harvest sparingly to avoid harming the tree.

CAUTION: Sassafras contains safrole, mainly in the root bark and leaves. Safrole has been linked to liver cancer in animals. The FDA has banned sassafras in commercial foods and drugs in the United States.

General Information

OTHER NAMES: Tapa cloth tree

HEIGHT: 33-66 feet (10–20 m) tall as a tree.

HABITATS: Thickets, mountain ravines, and forests

EDIBLE PARTS: Young leaves, fruits, flowers

60 Paper Mulberry
Broussonetia papyrifera

IDENTIFICATION FEATURES

BARK: The bark is light brown and slightly rough, often becoming fissured as the tree ages.

BRANCH/TWIG: Young twigs are slender, green to orange-brown, covered with tiny hairs, and have milky sap. As they mature, the color deepens to a brownish-gray. The branches are often spreading and slightly zigzag.

LEAF: Leaves are alternate and vary widely in shape even on the same tree - they can be heart-shaped, mitten-shaped, or deeply lobed. They measure about 4-10 inches (10-25 cm) long and wide, have a rough texture, and a toothed margin. The upper surface is dark green, while the lower is lighter and softly hairy.

FLOWER: The plant is a dioecious species, meaning male and female flowers grow on separate plants. Male flowers form in fuzzy catkins, while female flowers appear in spherical clusters, displaying long styles.

FRUIT: The tree bears fruit in distinctive clusters; each spherical cluster contains numerous small red or orange drupes.

SEED: The seeds are tiny, contained within the drupes that make up the fruit.

ODOR: When crushed, the leaves and twigs have a mild to strong odor often described as unpleasant.

EDIBLE USE: The young leaves can be cooked for consumption, typically by steaming or boiling. The fruits, though not overly abundant in the flesh, have an excellent flavor and can be gently cooked and incorporated into preserves or compotes, enhancing their unique taste. Additionally, the flowers of this plant can also be consumed.

MEDICINAL USE: The leaf juice is used as a diaphoretic, laxative, and for skin conditions; the fruit as a diuretic, stimulant, and tonic; and the root to promote lactation.

HARVESTING: Young leaves can be harvested as the plant grows, while fruits are collected when they mature to about 1.5 cm in diameter. It's best to harvest during dry conditions to minimize the risk of fungal growth.

CAUTION: Frequent fruit consumption might weaken bones. As always, before consuming or using any part of this plant medicinally, it's recommended to consult with a healthcare provider.

General Information

OTHER NAMES: Evening star, sundrop, fever plant, cure-all

HEIGHT: Up to 5.2 feet (1.6 m) tall

HABITATS: Fields, prairies, meadows, thickets, waste ground, disturbed sites, and along roadsides and railroad right-of-ways

EDIBLE PARTS: Roots, leaves, stems, flowers, seeds, and seed pods

61 Evening Primrose
Oenothera biennis

IDENTIFICATION FEATURES

STEM: Upright, hairy, reddish-green, can have multiple stems.

LEAF: Lanceolate, light green to olive green, 3-7 inches (8-18 cm) long and 0.8-2.4 inches (2-6 cm) wide. The leaves are shallow-toothed along the margins and stalkless or nearly so. The basal leaves form a rosette in the first year, while the stem leaves are spirally arranged in the second year.

FLOWER: Yellow flowers that are 1-2 inches (2.5-5 cm) across. The flowers have four petals that are notched at the tip. They also have four green sepals that bend backward at maturity. The flowers have eight yellow stamens and a long style with a cross-shaped stigma that protrudes beyond the petals.

FRUIT: It produces narrow seed pods that are long and hairy. The seed pods are capsules that split open when ripe to release numerous tiny brown seeds (up to 100 per capsule). The seeds are irregular and have a pitted surface.

SEED: Irregular and have a pitted surface.

ODOR: The flowers are lemon-scented.

EDIBLE USE: The plant offers edible roots, leaves, stems, flowers, and seeds. The roots can be boiled and eaten similarly to potatoes or sliced and stir-fried. They have a sweet, peppery flavor that pairs well with various dishes. The young leaves and stems can be cooked and used as a green or added raw to salads. The flower buds can be eaten raw or cooked like a vegetable, while its seeds, rich in gamma-linolenic acid, can be consumed directly or used to produce evening primrose oil, a supplement reputed for various health benefits. The young seed pods can be steamed or stir-fried.

MEDICINAL USE: Can treat various conditions such as eczema, arthritis, and menopause symptoms. It can also be used to induce labor and ripen the cervix in pregnant women, but always consult a doctor first.

HARVESTING: The leaves can be picked throughout the growing season but become tougher and more bitter as they mature. The roots can be dug up in late fall or early spring, when they are most tender and sweet. The seeds are collected from the capsules that form after the flowers fade.

CAUTION: Possible side effects include nausea, headaches, and low blood pressure. It can interact with certain medications. Not recommended for pregnant and breastfeeding women.

62 Fireweed
Chamerion angustifolium

General Information

OTHER NAMES: Great willowherb, bombweed

HEIGHT: 3-7 feet (0.9-2.1 m) tall

HABITATS: Open meadows, forest clearings, burn areas, and disturbed sites

EDIBLE PARTS: Young leaves, shoots, young flowers

IDENTIFICATION FEATURES

STEM: Upright, often reddish, primarily unbranched, with scattered alternate leaves and sometimes have stiff hairs on the upper part.

LEAF: Spirally arranged, willow-like leaves with circular veins that do not terminate at the leaf edges. Leaves are 2-6 inches (5-15 cm) long and 3/4 inches (1.9 cm) wide, with smooth margins and pointed tips. They are dark green above and paler below, with prominent veins and a creamy white midrib.

FLOWER: 1 inch (2.5 cm) across, with four petals that alternate with four narrow sepals. The petals are usually pink to purple, rarely white. The flowers have 8 stamens and a four-cleft stigma. The flowers are arranged in a raceme that is 3-8 inches (7.6-20 cm) long, with flowers blooming from bottom to top.

FRUIT: Cylindrical reddish-brown cap- sules, 1-2 inches (2.5-5 cm) long, splitting upon maturity to release seeds.

SEED: Tiny, brown seeds with silky hairs at one end.

EDIBLE USE: The young leaves and shoots, when cooked, serve as a nutritious green in soups and stews, or they can be steamed and served as a side dish. The leaves can also be dried and fermented into tea, which has a flavor somewhat reminiscent of black tea. The pink flowers add color and a slight sweetness to salads and can be used to make fireweed jelly or syrup, which have a unique, sweet-spicy flavor. Fireweed honey, made when bees collect nectar from its flowers, is a delicacy in regions where the plant is abundant.

MEDICINAL USE: Traditionally used for gastrointestinal issues like diarrhea and stomach pain, and externally for skin issues like burns and sores. It's also used for respiratory ailments like colds and bronchitis.

HARVESTING: The best time to pick fireweed is when the shoots are tender and not too woody. The flowers can be harvested throughout the summer and in early fall.

CAUTION: It may cause allergic reactions in some individuals. It can interac____ blood thinners or antidepressant_____sult a doctor before consuming it. _____suming large quantities of the plan_____ have a laxative effect.

63 Plantain
Plantago major

IDENTIFICATION FEATURES

STEM: Erect, unbranched, leafless, less than 12 inches (30.5 cm) tall.

LEAF: Oval to elliptic, with parallel veins and wavy margins. Usually green or pale at the base, but may have red or purple tinges near the petiole. The leaves are typically 2-8 inches (5-20 cm) long, 2-4 inches (5-10 cm) wide.

FLOWER: Small, greenish-brown with white to purple stamens, arranged in dense spikes at the end of the stalk.

FRUIT: Capsules that split open near the middle, releasing seeds that are oval, brown, and ridged. The fruits are 0.1-0.16 inches (2.5 to 4 mm) long.

SEED: Oval, brown, and ridged seeds.

EDIBLE USE: The plant is high in calcium and vitamins A, C, and K. The young leaves can be eaten raw in salads, offering a flavor somewhat akin to Swiss chard. They can also be cooked and used like spinach, adding a nutritious boost to dishes like soups, stews, and stir-fries. Older leaves, due to their fibrous texture, are best cooked or used to make plantain leaf tea, which is noted for its mild, herbaceous flavor. The seeds, a source of psyllium, can be ground into flour and used in baking or as a thickener in cooking.

MEDICINAL USE: It is used for wound healing and various diseases due to its anti-inflammatory properties. It can also soothe digestive problems and potentially slow down certain cancer cell growth.

HARVESTING: The plant grows throughout the year in most regions, but the best time to harvest it is in spring and summer when the leaves are young and tender. To harvest the leaves, cut them off at the base with a knife or scissors. To harvest the seeds, wait until the flower spikes turn brown and dry in late summer or fall. Then cut off the spikes and shake them over a paper bag or a bowl to collect the seeds.

CAUTION: It can lower blood pressure and interfere with blood clotting. Not recommended for people with hypotension, bleeding disorders, or on blood pressure medication.

OTHER NAMES: American speedwell

HEIGHT: 4-20 inches (10-50 cm) tall

HABITATS: Prefers wet habitats, such as shores of rivers or lakes, seeps, swamps, and margins of pools

EDIBLE PARTS: Leaves, stems, flowers

64 American Brooklime
Veronica americana

IDENTIFICATION FEATURES

STEM: Glabrous stems prostrate along the ground and root at the nodes, sending up vertical flowering stalks.

LEAF: Simple, opposite, and oval to lanceolate in shape. They have smooth or slightly toothed edges, and are glabrous on both surfaces. The leaves are green above and paler below. They are 0.5-3 inches (1.3-5.2 cm) long and 3 to 20 times as long as wide.

FLOWER: Small, about 1/3 inch (0.85 cm) across, and have four petals. The flowers are soft violet, sometimes with darker veins or white centers. The flowers have one or two stamens that protrude from the center.

FRUIT: The capsules have two valves that split open when ripe, releasing numerous tiny seeds.

SEED: Encased within a 2-lobed capsule fruit.

EDIBLE USE: The entire plant (except the roots) can be eaten raw or cooked, provided that the water source is not contaminated. The plant is rich in nutrients, such as vitamin C, iron, calcium, and potassium. The leaves and young shoots can be eaten raw in salads or cooked, adding a touch of green to soups, stews, and stir-fries. They can also be used to make a mild, refreshing tea. The plant's small blue flowers, though not rich in flavor, can be used as an edible garnish, adding a pop of color to salads and desserts.

MEDICINAL USE: It has been used for ailments like coughs, colds, sore throats, and skin infections due to its anti-inflammatory, antibacterial, and antitumor properties. It can be used in various forms like tea, tincture, or poultice.

HARVESTING: American brooklime blooms in summer, and can be harvested throughout growing season. The best time to pick the plant is when it is young and tender, before it becomes woody and bitter. To harvest the plant, cut or pull the stems near the base, leaving some roots and shoots for regrowth. Rinse the plant well to remove any dirt or insects, and use it fresh or store it in a cool, dry place.

CAUTION: Ensure it is collected from a clean source. Some people may be allergic to the plant. Pregnant or breastfeeding women should seek advice from a healthcare professional before use.

General Information

OTHER NAMES: Giant reed, phrag

HEIGHT: Up to 20 feet (6 m) tall

HABITATS: Wet or muddy ground along waterways. Roadsides, and agricultural fields

EDIBLE PARTS: Young stems, shoots, leaves, rhizomes, seeds, sap

65 Common Reed
Phragmites australis

IDENTIFICATION FEATURES

STEM: Hollow, erect, and cane-like, with ridges or ribs along their length.

LEAF: Linear to lanceolate, simple, alternate with pointed tips and tight sheaths. Measures 8-24 inches (20-60 cm) long and 0.4-2.4 inches (1-6 cm) wide.

FLOWER: Dark purple panicles (6-20 inches or 15-50 cm long) with wedge-shaped spikelets, each hosting small florets with fluffy bases and protective structures (glumes) at the base that are shorter than the spikelets.

FRUIT: Grain-like fruits (caryopsis) that turn gray in the fall.

SEED: Minute seeds dispersed via long, silky hairs.

ROOT: Can spread rapidly by horizontal runners, capable of rooting at intervals, forming extensive stands.

EDIBLE USES: Young stems and shoots can be consumed raw, cooked, pickled, or dried. They can be processed into a fine powder and, when mixed with water and roasted, produce a marshmallow-like substance. These shoots can also serve as a staple in stir-fry dishes, similar to bamboo shoots. The rhizomes can be eaten raw or cooked like potatoes, providing a hearty, starchy element to meals. The seeds, while time-consuming to collect, offer a nutritious option. The plant's sweet flavor, sometimes compared to licorice, is due to its high sugar content, and the sap from cut stems can be eaten raw or gently rolled to create edible candies.

MEDICINAL USE: Native American tribes used common reed for diarrhea, gastrointestinal issues, pain, cough, vomiting, and boils.

HARVESTING: Harvest the shoots in spring when young and tender, as they're most palatable then. Cut the stems near the base using a sharp tool and wear protective clothing to avoid potential skin irritation or allergies.

CAUTION: Generally safe to eat, but avoid if you have kidney problems or grass allergies.

POISONOUS LOOK-ALIKES: *Phalaris arundinacea* (reed canary grass)

• Leaves: Reed has wider, flat leaves, while canary grass has narrower, folded leaves.

• Inflorescence: Reed has dense, fluffy, purplish inflorescences while canary grass has compact, less showy, greenish to purple inflorescences.

Phalaris arundinacea

General Information

OTHER NAMES: Redshank

HEIGHT: Up to 3.3 feet (1 m) tall

HABITATS: Damp meadows, shores, roadsides, and disturbed areas

EDIBLE PARTS: Young leaves, shoots, seeds

66 Lady's Thumb
Polygonum persicaria

IDENTIFICATION FEATURES

STEM: Erect or ascending, often reddish-green, simple or branched.

LEAF: Alternate, lance-shaped to elliptic, and usually have a dark purple blotch on the upper surface. The leaves are 2-4 inches (5-10 cm) long and 1/3 to 1 inch (0.85-2.5 cm) wide, with smooth margins and pointed tips. The upper surface of the leaves is dark green, while the lower surface is paler green and sometimes hairy.

FLOWER: Small, pink to purple or sometimes white, and lacks petals. They are arranged in dense spikes at the end of the stems or in the leaf axils. The flowers usually have 6 stamens and a style that protrudes from the sepal tube. The flowers are grouped in dense spikes, 0.4-1.6 inches (1-4 cm) long.

FRUIT: Achenes that are 0.08-0.12 inches (2-3 mm) long. They are shiny black and triangular in cross-section, surrounded by a thin papery perianth.

SEED: The seed is the fruit (achene) itself.

EDIBLE USE: The young leaves and shoots are tender and mild, whereas the older ones are tougher and less flavorful. The leaves can be utilized in salads, or cooked in soups, stews, and stir-fries. They can also be lightly sautéed in butter or olive oil with garlic and served as a side dish. Although the seeds can be harvested and eaten, they are quite small and cumbersome to use. Polygonum persicaria has a high content of natural sugars, fiber, phenolic acids, and tannins.

MEDICINAL USE: It is a traditional remedy for digestive and urinary problems. The flowering stems can be brewed into tea to soothe stomach pain, diarrhea, bleeding, and urinary infections.

HARVESTING: Lady's thumb can be found from spring to fall, but the best time to harvest it is when the plant is young and tender. The seed (achene) can be harvested following the flowering period. To harvest the plant, simply cut or pinch off the leaves and shoots from the stem. Wash the plant well before using it.

CAUTION: It contains oxalic acid, which can interfere with calcium absorption and cause kidney stones in large amounts. Consume in moderation and avoid daily intake. It may also cause photosensitivity, so avoid sunlight exposure after consumption.

67 Knotweed
Polygonum aviculare

IDENTIFICATION FEATURES

STEM: Knotweed has a sprawling, mat-forming growth habit with multiple branching stems that are often green or reddish-brown.

LEAF: The leaves are alternate, narrow, oblong, or lance-shaped, measuring up to 1 inch (2.5 cm) long and 1/3 inch (0.85 cm) wide. They have a smooth margin and a short petiole, and a sheath (ocrea) surrounds the leaf base where it attaches to the stem.

FLOWER: Knotweed flowers are small, greenish-white to pink, and inconspicuous, located in the leaf axils along the stems. They have five tepals (where petals and sepals are indistinguishable).

FRUIT: The fruits are small, brown, three-sided achenes that are less than 1 inch (2.5 cm) in size and enclosed by persistent tepals.

SEED: Small, black to reddish-brown seeds. These seeds are triangular in cross-section and have a flattened, lens-like shape.

EDIBLE USE: The young leaves can be eaten raw in salads or cooked in a similar way to spinach. The seeds can be dried out and then ground into flour. This can be a meticulous process, but it is often worth the effort. The resulting flour is versatile - it can be incorporated into baking recipes to make bread, cakes, and pastries or as a thickening agent in soups and stews.

MEDICINAL USE: It has been used traditionally in treating gastrointestinal issues, respiratory problems, and skin conditions.

HARVESTING: The best time to harvest knotweed is when the young leaves are tender. Collect the leaves by pinching or cutting them from the plant, being careful not to damage the rest of the plant.

POISONOUS LOOK-ALIKES: *Euphorbia maculata* (spotted spurge) has toxic milky sap.

• Leaves: *P. aviculare* has narrow, pointed leaves arranged alternately or sometimes oppositely, while *E. maculata* has ovate, oppositely arranged leaves with a red spot in the middle.

• Stems: *P. aviculare* has rounded stems, while *E. maculata* has reddish, prostrate stems that produce a milky sap when broken.

Euphorbia maculata

OTHER NAMES: Woodland strawberry, Alpine strawberry

HEIGHT: 2-8 inches (5 to 20 cm) tall

HABITATS: Woodlands, meadows, fields, roadsides, clearings, and waste areas

EDIBLE PARTS: Fruits, leaves

68 Wild Strawberry
Fragaria vesca

IDENTIFICATION FEATURES

STEM: The plant has slender stolons (runners) that spread horizontally and produce new plants.

LEAF: The leaves are composed of three leaflets that are oval or obovate in shape, up to 1.5 inches (3.8 cm) long, with toothed margins and prominent veins. The leaflets are sparsely hairy on both surfaces. The terminal leaflet is larger than the lateral ones and has a wedge-shaped base.

FLOWER: The flowers are white, with five rounded petals. The petals are separate and not fused at the base. The flowers have many yellow stamens that surround a pistil with multiple styles. The flowers are borne on slender stalks that arise from the leaf axils or the tips of the stolons. The flowers sometimes form clusters of 2 to 5.

FRUIT: The fruits are small, red berries that have a conical or spherical shape. They are covered with tiny seeds (achenes). The fruits have a sweet and aromatic flavor that varies depending on the variety and growing conditions.

SEED: Tiny seeds (achenes) that are embedded in the surface of the juicy part (receptacle) of the fruit.

EDIBLE USE: Wild strawberry produces small, aromatic fruits that can be eaten fresh or dried. The fruits are rich in vitamin C, antioxidants, and flavonoids. They can be added to salads, or used in desserts like cakes, pies, and tarts. Their sweet-tart flavor complements both sweet and savory dishes, from strawberry shortcakes and ice creams to salads and gourmet main dishes. Wild strawberries can also be made into preserves, jellies, syrups, and wines. Additionally, their dried leaves can be used to make a flavorful tea.

MEDICINAL USE: Used in traditional medicine for various purposes: The leaves make a Vitamin C-rich tea that aids digestion. It treats gout, rheumatism, and night sweats.

HARVESTING: Wild strawberry is an ever-bearing plant that produces flowers and fruits throughout the growing season. The best time to pick the fruits is when they are fully ripe and red. The fruits can be easily detached from the stems by hand or with a knife.

CAUTION: It is generally safe to eat, but some people may be allergic to the fruits or leaves. Allergic reactions may include itching, swelling, rash, hives, or difficulty breathing. Seek medical attention if these symptoms occur.

69 American Plum
Prunus americana

IDENTIFICATION FEATURES

BARK: Begins as smooth, reddish-gray with horizontal breathing pores (lenticels), becoming rough and ridged with age.

STEM: It has dark reddish-brown branches and twigs that sometimes have thorny branchlets.

LEAF: The leaves are alternately arranged, ovate, toothed with a pointed tip, and 3-4 inches (7.6-10 cm) long. They are dark green in summer and turn yellow to red in autumn.

FLOWER: The flowers are white, 5-petaled, and 1 inch (2.5 cm) in diameter. They appear in clusters of 2-5 (umbels) in March before the foliage. They are unpleasantly aromatic.

FRUIT: The flowers are followed by edible round red plums about 1 inch (2.5 cm) in diameter and have bright yellow pulp.

EDIBLE USE: Fruits can be eaten fresh, used in baked goods like pies, crumbles, and cakes, or made into jams, jellies, and preserves. The plums can also be stewed and eaten as a topping for ice cream or yogurt. They can be dried for long-term storage and then rehydrated and used in a variety of recipes. The

General Information

OTHER NAMES: Wild plum

HEIGHT: Up to 15 feet (4.6 m) tall

HABITATS: Prairies, pastures, woodlands, and along stream banks and roadsides

EDIBLE PARTS: Fruits

sweet-tart flavor of these plums also makes them suitable for use in savory dishes, where they can be used in sauces, chutneys, or as an accompaniment to meats.

MEDICINAL USE: It has been used by Native Americans for various medicinal purposes. The bark was a tonic, astringent, and antiseptic. The roots treated wounds, ulcers, and boils. The fruits addressed diarrhea, dysentery, and fever.

HARVESTING: The best time to pick the fruits of American plum is when they are fully ripe from early summer onwards. They can be easily plucked from the branches or shaken off the tree. The fruits should be washed and processed as soon as possible after harvesting to prevent spoilage and insect damage.

CAUTION: The seeds, leaves, and stems contain cyanogenic glycosides that release cyanide when chewed or crushed. Avoid or remove these parts before consuming the fruits.

General Information

OTHER NAMES: European red raspberry

HEIGHT: 5-8 feet (1.5–2.5 m) tall

HABITATS: Forest edges, meadows, fields, shrublands, wetlands, and disturbed areas

EDIBLE PARTS: Leaves, fruits

The fruits are juicy, sweet, and edible.

EDIBLE USE: The plant has edible berries. It is a common ingredient in desserts such as pies, tarts, and cheesecakes due to its sweet yet slightly tart flavor. It can also be used to make jellies, jams, and preserves, providing a burst of fruity flavor to breakfast dishes and desserts. Raspberry coulis, a smooth sauce made from pureed and strained raspberries, is a delicious addition to sweet and savory dishes. Raspberries can also be used in beverages, from refreshing raspberry-infused water to cocktails and non-alcoholic spritzers. They also freeze well for later use in smoothies or baked goods. The leaves can also be used to make herbal teas that have medicinal properties.

MEDICINAL USE: The leaves and roots are used to treat diarrhea, dysentery, sore throat, mouth ulcers, bleeding gums, wounds, menstrual problems, and childbirth complications. The leaves contain antioxidants and have anti-inflammatory properties.

HARVESTING: The best time to pick red raspberry is when the fruits are ripe and juicy. To harvest the fruits, gently pull them from the receptacle (the white part holding them) without crushing them. To harvest the leaves, cut the stems with a sharp knife or scissors.

CAUTION: It is generally safe to eat, but some may have allergies or digestive issues. The plant has spines or thorns that can cause skin irritation.

70 Red Raspberry
Rubus idaeus

IDENTIFICATION FEATURES

STEM: The plant has spines or prickles along their length, which help them to climb over other plants or structures. Leaf stalks have gland-tipped hairs.

LEAF: The leaves are composed of three to five leaflets. These leaflets are usually ovate, serrated along the edges, and have a white, felt-like underside due to a dense covering of tiny hairs.

FLOWER: The flowers are arranged in clusters at the ends of the branches or along the canes. They have five petals that are white or pink, five sepals that are green or reddish, and many stamens and pistils.

FRUIT: The fruits are aggregate drupes, which consist of many small fleshy drupelets.

OTHER NAMES: Dewberry

HEIGHT: Up to 5 feet (1.5 m) tall, but can occasionally reach over 8 feet (2.4 m)

HABITATS: Forest edges, roadsides, fields, pastures, and disturbed areas

EDIBLE PARTS: Young shoots, fruits

71 Allegheny Blackberry
Rubus allegheniensis

IDENTIFICATION FEATURES

BARK: purple-red, with prickles.

STEM: The canes start as green and mature into a reddish-brown color, with many prickles present. It is also characterized by having gland-tipped hairs on the branches of the inflorescence.

LEAF: The leaves are green on both sides, with a smooth or slightly hairy surface. The leaflets are oval to elliptic, with pointed tips and rounded or heart-shaped bases. The margins are coarsely serrated or doubly serrated. The leaflets are 2-6 inches (5-15 cm) long and 1-4 inches (2.5-10 cm) wide.

FLOWER: The flowers are white, with five petals that are about 0.75 inch (1.9 cm) long and wide. The flowers have numerous stamens and green pistils. The flowers are arranged in clusters at the branches' ends or leaf axils.

FRUIT: The fruit is a black aggregate fruit about 0.4 inch (1 cm) in diameter, composed of small drupelets. The fruits are ripe when they turn red to black and detach easily from the receptacle.

EDIBLE USE: The fruits are excellent for fresh eating and can also be used in an array of culinary applications. They can be baked into pies, tarts, and muffins, or used to make flavorful jams, jellies, and sauces. Blackberry coulis, a sauce made from pureed and strained blackberries, can elevate desserts and savory dishes. Blackberries also pair well with a variety of cheeses, making them a great addition to cheese boards. For beverage enthusiasts, blackberries can be used to create refreshing infused waters, cocktails, and homemade wines. The young shoots can be eaten as well, either raw or cooked, but they are more bitter than the fruits.

MEDICINAL USE: It has been used by Native Americans for various medicinal purposes. The root bark acts as a diuretic, astringent, and tonic. The leaves treat diarrhea, dysentery, sore throat, mouth ulcers, eye irritation, and skin problems. The fruits address scurvy, anemia, and infections.

HARVESTING: The fruits should be picked before they become overripe and soft, as they may spoil quickly or attract insects. The fruits can be kept in the refrigerator for a few days or frozen for longer periods.

CAUTION: It is generally safe to eat, but some may have allergies or digestive issues. Cook young shoots and leaves to neutralize oxalic acid, which can cause kidney stones.

72 Woods' Rose
Rosa woodsii

OTHER NAMES: Common wild rose, mountain rose, pear-hip rose

HEIGHT: 3-6 feet (0.9-1.8 m) tall

HABITATS: Open woods, plains, stream banks, and disturbed areas

EDIBLE PARTS: Young shoots, stems, flowers, fruits

IDENTIFICATION FEATURES

STEM: The stems are straight, red to grey-brown, and studded with prickles.

LEAF: The leaves are deep green, alternate, and pinnately compound with 5-9 leaflets that are widely spaced and serrated on the upper part. The leaflets are up to 2 inches (5 cm) long and oval or elliptic in shape.

FLOWER: The flowers are very fragrant and have five petals in any shade of pink, and are up to 1 inch (2.5 cm) in length. They have many stamens and pistils and are borne in small cymes of up to a few flowers.

FRUIT: The fruits of Rosa woodsii are fleshy, red rose hips that may be over 0.4 inches (1 cm) long. They are round or pear-shaped and persist on the bush throughout the winter.

EDIBLE USE: The rose hips (fruits) can be used to make jellies, jams, syrups, pies, and even homemade wines. Rose hip tea is also popular due to its high vitamin C content and distinct flavor. Rose hips can be dried for long-term storage and used later in baking, sauces, or steeped to make tea. The petals are also edible and can be used to add color and a subtle floral flavor to salads, desserts, and drinks. They can also be crystallized and used as a beautiful garnish on cakes and pastries. The young shoots and stems can also be eaten raw (peeled) or cooked as a vegetable, or added to salads.

MEDICINAL USE: Woods' rose hips have been used by Native American tribes for treating colds, flu, sore throat, diarrhea, and infections, as well as a tonic and anti-inflammatory. The flower petals treat eye problems, skin problems, and headaches. The bark and roots treat wounds, ulcers, rheumatism, and toothache.

HARVESTING: The best time to pick the plant is when the flowers are in full bloom or when the hips are ripe. To harvest the flowers, cut them off with scissors or a knife at the base of the stem. To harvest the hips, cut them off with scissors or a knife at the stem or twist them off by hand. Be careful of the prickles on the stems and leaves.

CAUTION: Woods' rose hips contain small seeds that may irritate the mouth and digestive tract if swallowed. Remove the seeds before consumption. Some people may be allergic to Woods' rose or its products, leading to skin rashes, itching, swelling, or breathing difficulties.

73 Common Hawthorn
Crataegus monogyna

General Information

OTHER NAMES: One-seed hawthorn

HEIGHT: Up to 33 feet (10 m) tall

HABITATS: Hedgerows, woodlands, and open fields

EDIBLE PARTS: Young leaves, flowers, fruits

IDENTIFICATION FEATURES

BARK: Dull brown with vertical cracks; Smooth and gray when young, and develops ridges with age.

BRANCH: Dense and alternate branching with sharp thorns.

LEAF: Dark green, broadly ovate, 1-2 inches (2.5-5 cm) long, with 3-7 deep lobes and serrated edges.

FLOWER: White or pale pink, about 0.5 inches (1.3 cm) across, grow in clusters; they have five petals and numerous stamens; bloom in spring.

FRUIT: Called haws, small, red, and oval, measuring 0.2-0.4 inches (0.5-1 cm) in diameter; ripen in late summer to early fall and persist on the tree into winter.

SEED: Contained within the fruit, dispersed by birds in their droppings.

EDIBLE USE: The haws can be eaten raw or cooked, though they are best after the first frost. They can be used to make jellies, wines, and ketchup, offering a mild apple-like flavor. The haws can be dried and ground into a flour substitute or used in baked goods. Young leaves and flower buds can be eaten raw in salads or cooked. They've also been used historically to make a fermented beverage. It's worth noting that the seeds inside the haws should not be consumed as they contain cyanide precursors.

MEDICINAL USE: It has been used in herbal medicine for treating heart conditions, high blood pressure, and digestive issues. It's also reported to have anti-inflammatory and antioxidant properties.

HARVESTING: The best time to harvest hawthorn leaves and flowers is in spring when the flowers are in full bloom. The fruits (haws) should be picked when they have ripened to a bright red color. It's essential to harvest the fruits after they've fully matured for optimal flavor and nutritional content.

CAUTION: Although hawthorn is generally considered safe, it may interact with certain medications, particularly those used for heart conditions. Consult a healthcare professional before using Hawthorn medicinally.

74 Saskatoon Berry
Amelanchier alnifolia

numerous long stamens with yellow anthers. They bloom in early spring to summer, often before the leaves fully emerge.

FRUIT: The fruits, known as pomes, are small, round berries that are initially green, ripening to a dark purplish-black. They are about 1/4-1/2 inch (6-13 mm) in diameter.

EDIBLE USE: Saskatoon berry has sweet, nutty fruits and is similar to blueberries. These berries can be eaten fresh or used in various dishes, such as pies, tarts, crumbles, jams, and jellies. They can also be dried for later use or made into juice. The berries can also be dried as a raisin substitute in baked goods or trail mixes. Additionally, the Saskatoon berries can be used to make wines and other alcoholic beverages.

MEDICINAL USE: The bark is traditionally used as an astringent and antidiarrheal agent, while the root is used for treating colds and flu.

HARVESTING: The best time to harvest Saskatoon berry is mid to late summer when the berries have ripened and turned a deep purplish-blue color. To harvest, gently pluck the berries from the branches, not crushing them.

CAUTION: Saskatoon berry are generally safe to eat, but consuming large quantities may cause mild gastrointestinal upset in some individuals. Also, avoid eating unripe berries, as they may contain small amounts of hydrogen cyanide.

IDENTIFICATION FEATURES

BARK: Smooth and gray to reddish-brown, sometimes with vertical fissures in older plants.

BRANCH: Generally slender, often taking on the same color as the bark.

LEAVES: The leaves are simple, alternate, and ovate or round in shape. They measure about 1-2 inches (2.5-5 cm) in length. The leaf edges have fine, sharp teeth, especially towards the tip. The upper surface of the leaves is medium to dark green and smooth, while the undersurface is paler and can have a slightly hairy texture, particularly along the veins. The leaves often turn a brilliant yellow or red in the fall.

FLOWER: The flowers bloom in clusters called racemes. Each flower is about 0.8 inch (2 cm) in diameter, with five white petals and

General Information

OTHER NAMES: Sweetscented bedstraw

HEIGHT: 12-20 inches (30–50 cm) long

HABITATS: Deciduous woodlands, forest edges, and shaded meadows

EDIBLE PARTS: Leaves, stems, flowers

75 Sweet Woodruff
Galium odoratum

IDENTIFICATION FEATURES

STEM: The stem is slender, square-shaped, and aromatic. It often roots at the nodes and can spread widely.

LEAF: Leaves are simple, whorled, with 6-9 leaves per whorl. They are 0.8-2 inches (2-5 cm) long, lanceolate to elliptical in shape, and dark green in color with a slightly rough texture and smooth edges. They exude a fragrance when crushed or dried.

FLOWER: The flowers are small (0.16-0.28 inches or 4-7 mm in diameter), with four petals, star-shaped, and white. They grow in loose clusters and have a strong, sweet fragrance.

FRUIT: Small, round, covered with hooked bristles. It is initially green, turning brown when ripe.

SEED: The seeds are small and dark, found within the capsule.

EDIBLE USE: Sweet woodruff has a sweet, hay-like flavor that intensifies when dried. It's famously used in Germany to flavor May Wine, a traditional springtime drink. The leaves, stems, and flowers can be used to flavor other beverages, like teas and fruit punches, or to infuse the milk for custards and other desserts. Dried leaves, due to their strong aroma, are also used in potpourris. While not commonly consumed in large amounts, sweet woodruff's distinct flavor profile can add a unique touch to culinary creations.

MEDICINAL USE: It has been traditionally used to treat various ailments, including digestive issues, liver problems, and insomnia. It is also known for its mild sedative and anti-inflammatory properties.

HARVESTING: The best time to harvest sweet woodruff is during the spring and summer when the plant is in full bloom. To harvest, cut the entire plant, including leaves, flowers, and stems, just above the ground level, taking care not to damage the roots.

CAUTION: Consuming in large quantities can cause headaches, dizziness, and vomiting. It is best to use it in moderation. Pregnant and breastfeeding women should avoid consuming sweet woodruff.

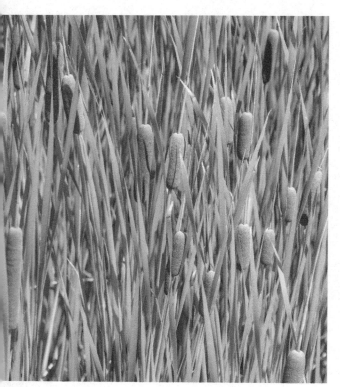

OTHER NAMES: Broadleaf cattail, bulrush

HEIGHT: 5-10 feet (1.5 to 3 m) tall

HABITATS: Grows in saturated soils and shallow water of lake shores, river shores, marshes, and ditches

EDIBLE PARTS: Young shoots, stems, lower parts of the leaves, flowers, pollen, rhizomes

are formed by the pollinated female flowers on the lower part of the inflorescence. The fruits form a cylindrical, sausage-like shape that usually persists until winter before disintegrating.

EDIBLE USES: Young shoots can be harvested and prepared like asparagus, requiring extended cooking time for tenderness, or consumed raw. The stems, too, can be eaten raw or boiled. The lower parts of the leaves find use in salads, adding a fresh, crisp element. As the plant matures, its flower spikes can be boiled, buttered, and enjoyed much like corn on the cob. The yellow pollen of the male flowers is an excellent addition to pancakes or bread when mixed with flour. The roots can be cleaned, boiled, baked, broiled, or even dried and processed into nutritious flour. This versatility has earned the cattail the moniker of "nature's supermarket".

MEDICINAL USE: It has been used traditionally for medicinal purposes, primarily as a poultice for cuts, burns, sores, and bruises due to its antibacterial properties. It has also been used as a blood purifier.

HARVESTING: The rhizomes can be harvested in winter and spring. The pollen can be collected in summer when the male flowers are shedding. The flower spikes can be picked in spring and summer when they are still green and soft.

76 Cattail
Typha latifolia

IDENTIFICATION FEATURES

STEM: The plant has a stiff, unbranched, and round central flower stalk that usually rises equal to or slightly less than the height of the leaves.

LEAF: Cattail has narrow, upright, sword-like, linear, mostly basal, green leaves that can be up to 8 feet (2.4 m) long.

FLOWER: The plant has minute flowers densely packed into a cylindrical inflorescence that can be up to 9 inches (23 cm) long. The male flowers are located at the top of the inflorescence, while the female flowers are located underneath. The male flowers disperse after pollination, leaving a naked stalk tip above the female flowers.

FRUIT: The plant has brown fruits that

General Information

OTHER NAMES: Common nettle, burn nettle, nettle leaf, stinger

HEIGHT: 3-7 feet (0.9-2 m) tall

HABITATS: Moist sites along streams, meadows, ditches, mountain slopes, and disturbed areas

EDIBLE PARTS: Young leaves, young shoots

77 Stinging Nettle
Urtica dioica

IDENTIFICATION FEATURES

STEM: The stem is usually unbranched, squarish in cross-section, and covered with small, stiff, stinging hairs that can cause skin irritation when touched.

LEAF: The leaves are opposite along the stem, 1-6 inches (2.5-15 cm) long, dark green, and oval to lance-shaped with pointed tips. The edges are coarsely toothed. Like the stem, the leaves also contain stinging hairs.

FLOWER: The plant has separate male and female flowers. The small, greenish, or white-pinkish flowers are arranged in elongated clusters that hang from the leaf axils.

FRUITS: The fruits are small and egg-shaped. They are green when young, turning brown as they mature.

SEEDS: The seeds are tiny, brown, and enclosed within the small fruit.

ODOR: When fresh, the plant has a distinct, somewhat unpleasant smell that some describe as fishy or pungent. The odor is less noticeable when the plant is dried.

EDIBLE USE: Stinging nettle is a versatile edible plant. Its young leaves, akin to spinach in taste when cooked, can be incorporated into numerous dishes. They serve as delightful additions to soups, a twist in polenta, or a unique ingredient for pesto. These greens can also be simmered and used as filling for pastries in diverse cuisines, from Balkan to Greek. Drying the young leaves allows for a refreshing herbal tea. Stinging nettle is even used to create certain cheeses and alcoholic beverages.

MEDICINAL USE: Nettle has applications in traditional medicine as a cleansing tonic and blood purifier. It is used to treat hay fever, arthritis, and anemia. It is applied externally to treat skin complaints. The root is beneficial for enlarged prostate glands.

HARVESTING: Once the plant starts to flower and set seeds, it develops gritty particles known as cystoliths which can be irritating if consumed. Therefore, leaves harvested after flowering should undergo a process such as fermentation to break down these cystoliths. It is advised to wear gloves when harvesting to avoid the plant's sting.

CAUTION: Consuming old leaves can cause laxative effects. After the plant flowers and sets seeds, the leaves develop cystoliths which can irritate the urinary tract and kidneys.

78 Common Blue Violet
Viola sororia

IDENTIFICATION FEATURES

STEM: Stems are relatively short, rhizomatous.

LEAF: The leaves are heart-shaped with a rounded or slightly pointed tip and are usually 1-3 inches (2.5-7.5 cm) long. The leaf margins can be smooth or slightly scalloped.

FLOWER: The flowers are blue-purple to purplish-white with five petals. The two lateral petals spread with white hairs at the base, while the bottom petal features a white center with darker purple veins.

FRUIT: The fruit is a 3-chambered capsule containing numerous seeds. The capsule splits open to release the seeds when the fruit matures.

SEED: The seeds of common blue violet are tiny and usually brown. They're ejected from the fruit capsule when it splits open, which helps to distribute the seeds away from the parent plant.

EDIBLE USE: The leaves can be eaten raw in salads, cooked as a green, or used to thicken soups due to their high mucilage content. The flowers, with their slightly sweet taste, can be used to make syrups, jellies, and beverages, or simply tossed into salads for a touch of color. They can also be candied and used as beautiful cake decorations. The flower petals can also be steeped in hot water to create a sweet-tasting tea.

MEDICINAL USE: Traditionally, the plant has been used for its mild expectorant and diuretic properties. Some people also use it as a mild pain reliever to soothe skin irritations.

HARVESTING: Leaves are edible and can be harvested throughout their growing period, usually in spring and summer. Flowers, also edible, are typically harvested in spring to early summer when in full bloom.

General Information

OTHER NAMES: Common meadow violet, purple violet

HEIGHT: Up to 3-8 inches (7.6-20 cm) tall

HABITATS: Lawns, gardens, woodlands, and meadows

EDIBLE PARTS: Leaves, flowers

General Information

OTHER NAMES: Frost grape, winter grape

HEIGHT: Climbing vine can grow up to 32 feet (10 m)

HABITATS: Moist and sunny habitats, such as riverbanks, floodplains, forests, and roadsides

EDIBLE PARTS: Leaves, fruits

79 Riverbank Grape
Vitis riparia

IDENTIFICATION FEATURES

BARK: Reddish-brown, exfoliating in long strips.

STEM: Yellowish-green to reddish, smooth branches. Riverbank grape uses its tendrils to climb over other plants. It has forked tendrils that wrap around supports. Mature trunk may have a diameter of up to 8 inches (20 cm).

LEAF: The leaves are alternate, simple, and hand-shaped (palmately lobed), with toothed margins and a heart-shaped base. They are usually dark green on the upper surface and lighter green on the lower surface, with some hairs along the veins.

FLOWER: The flowers are small, greenish-white, and fragrant, arranged in clusters called panicles.

FRUIT: The fruits are small, round berries that turn from green to purple-black when ripe. They are 1/4 to 1/2 inch (0.6-1.3 cm) in diameter, have a sour taste, and contain seeds.

EDIBLE USE: Riverbank grape produces small, tart grapes that can be used in various culinary applications. They can be made into jams, jellies, and preserves or used to make grape juice or wine. The grapes can also be baked into pies, tarts, and crumbles. For a unique culinary experience, try pickling the grapes or using them in savory sauces to accompany meat dishes. The leaves are also edible and are often used in the traditional dish dolmas, where they are stuffed with rice and various fillings.

MEDICINAL USE: The bark is used for treating chronic diarrhea and dysentery. The leaves can be used externally for treating sore eyes, while the sap is sometimes used for skin issues.

HARVESTING: The best time to harvest riverbank grapes is in summer or fall, when they are fully ripe and have a sweet flavor. The grapes can be easily picked by hand or with scissors, but be careful of the potential presence of insects or diseases.

CAUTION: Avoid eating unripe or overripe grapes, which may cause stomach upset or diarrhea. You should also be aware of possible allergic reactions or interactions with medications, especially if you have a history of grape allergy or sensitivity.

80 Orange Daylily
Hemerocallis fulva

IDENTIFICATION FEATURES

STEM: The plant has leafless flower stems (scapes) reaching up to 4 feet (1.2 m) tall. These stems are round in cross-section and upright.

LEAF: The leaves are long, flat, and strap-like, arranged in a fan shape at the base of the plant. They are bright green and grow up to 3 feet (0.9 m) long.

FLOWER: The flowers are large, showy, and funnel-shaped, up to 4 inches (10 cm) across. They typically have 6 orange tepals (3 petals and 3 sepals similar in appearance), often with a darker orange or brownish central stripe. Each flower blooms for only one day, but each stem produces several flowers which open in succession.

FRUIT: After flowering, the plant forms a three-parted capsule fruit, about an inch (2.5 cm) long, containing numerous black seeds.

ODOR: Daylilies generally have a mild, sweet fragrance, although the strength of the scent can vary between different varieties. The fragrance is often more noticeable in the early morning or late evening.

EDIBLE USE: Orange daylily is a versatile culinary ingredient that has been a part of East Asian cuisines for centuries. The young leaves, spring shoots, and unopened flower buds are often harvested and stir-fried, steamed, or used in soups and salads. The flowers, both fresh and dried, add a unique, slightly sweet, and floral flavor to dishes and can be stuffed, battered, and fried. Additionally, the tubers are edible and can be eaten raw or cooked like a root vegetable. They have a nutty flavor and are often used as a potato substitute.

MEDICINAL USE: It has been used in traditional Chinese medicine. It is believed to have a cooling effect and is used to treat insomnia, anxiety, and depression. It's also used for detoxification and treating swelling.

HARVESTING: Orange daylily should be harvested when the leaves, shoots, and flower buds are still young, as they can become fibrous and less palatable with age. Flowers can be harvested when they are somewhat withered and closed if they are to be dried and used as a soup thickener. Tubers are best when young, although the central portion of older tubers can still be consumed.

CAUTION: Consumption of large quantities of the leaves can reportedly cause hallucinogenic effects. This component can be removed by blanching the leaves.

EDIBLE MUSHROOMS

General Information

OTHER NAMES: Field mushroom, pink bottom

SIZE: Cap 1-4.8 inches (3-12 cm) in diameter, stipe 1-4 inches (3-10 cm) tall

HABITATS: Grassy areas, meadows, pastures (sometimes in fairy rings)

EDIBLE PARTS: The whole fruiting body

81 Meadow Mushroom
Agaricus campestris

IDENTIFICATION: Look for white to light brown cap and pink to chocolate-brown gills.

CAP: Smooth, white to light brown surface, may have fine scales; convex to broadly convex, like a dome or an umbrella, occasionally nearly flat.

GILLS: Crowded like thin blades, deep pink at first, then red-brown, and finally dark chocolate brown, not attaching to the stipe.

STIPE: Cylindrical, solid stipe with a thin, fragile ring.

FLESH: White in color, bruises reddish brown.

SPORE PRINT: Dark brown.

ODOR: Mild and pleasant.

EDIBLE USE: Mild and earthy flavor, firm texture; suitable for various dishes. It can be sautéed, fried, grilled, baked, roasted, stuffed, or added to soups, salads, sauces, casseroles, pies, omelets, pizzas, sandwiches, and burgers. Also used to make mushroom ketchup, a popular 18th and 19th-century condiment.

HARVESTING: Fruits from summer to early winter, depending on climate and rainfall. Best picked when the cap is still convex, and the gills are pink. Use a knife to cut the stipe at the base, or gently twist the mushroom from the ground to minimize disturbance to mycelium.

POISONOUS LOOK-ALIKES: *Agaricus xanthodermus* (mildly toxic). Differentiate by:

• Yellow staining: *A. xanthodermus* turns bright yellow when bruised or cut, especially at the stipe base; *A. campestris* doesn't.

• Odor: *A. xanthodermus* has an unpleasant, phenolic or ink-like odor; *A. campestris* is mild and mushroom-like.

• Cap: *A. xanthodermus* often has a slightly scaly cap; *A. campestris* is smooth.

• Habitats: *A. xanthodermus* found in wood chips, gardens, or disturbed soil; *A. campestris* in grassy areas.

Agaricus xanthodermus

82 Horse Mushroom
Agaricus arvensis

IDENTIFICATION FEATURES

CAP: White to cream-colored, slightly convex to flat with age, stains yellow, especially when young; the smooth surface may develop brownish scales as it ages.

GILLS: Crowded, free from the stipe, pale pink to dark brown with age.

STIPE: Thick, club-shaped, with a large, movable, membranous ring; the upper layer of the ring is white, and the lower layer may have yellowish scales and a distinct "cogwheel" pattern, especially in young, closed-cap mushrooms.

FLESH: Thick, white, slightly yellow when cut or bruised, but doesn't stain strongly.

SPORE PRINT: Chocolate brown.

ODOR: Pleasant, with a slight anise-like aroma.

EDIBLE USE: Known for its mild, almond-like flavor, this mushroom can be used as a substitute for white button or portobello mushrooms in recipes. It can be sautéed with garlic and herbs, grilled for a smoky taste, or stuffed with a mix of cheese and breadcrumbs. It also works well in quiches, pasta sauces, and stir-fries, adding a delicious depth of flavor to any meal. Cooking is required to avoid stomach upset or allergic reactions.

HARVESTING: Fruits from mid-summer to late fall; choose young, fresh specimens with closed or just-opening caps; cut stipe at the base with a knife without disturbing surrounding mycelium.

CAUTION: Cook thoroughly, and avoid collection from polluted areas; it may cause gastrointestinal upset if raw or undercooked.

POISONOUS LOOK-ALIKES: *Agaricus xanthodermus* (page 114) and *Chlorophyllum molybdites*.

• *A. arvensis*: Anise-like or almond-like aroma for differentiation.

• *C. molybdites*: Greenish spores, gills turn greenish with age, unlike pinkish to chocolate-brown gills of *A. arvensis*.

Chlorophyllum molybdites

83 The Prince
Agaricus augustus

IDENTIFICATION: The prince is large, easily recognizable with distinct features.

CAP: Features a large cap that transitions from hemispherical to convex and finally flat; yellow-brown to dark brown, dry surface with brown scales on a white to yellow background.

GILLS: Crowded, pale initially, turning pink then dark brown as they mature; free from stipe; young mushrooms have a thin white partial veil (protective covering) with small darker warts (bumps), connecting stipe to cap edge.

STIPE: Club-shaped, possibly with a narrow central hollow; pendulous ring remaining on stipe after partial veil tears; stipe is white to yellow and smooth above the ring, and covered with small scales below.

FLESH: Thick, white, firm flesh that may turn yellow when bruised.

SPORE PRINT: Brown.

ODOR: Pleasant, almond-like scent.

EDIBLE USE: Highly prized for its distinct nutty taste, this mushroom is a delightful addition to various dishes, such as risottos, stews, and soups. It can be prepared by sautéing for a rich, savory flavor, which pairs well with

meats, vegetables, or pasta. It is also a great topping for pizza or can be fried with butter and salt, grilled with olive oil and salt or BBQ sauce, and even used in a mushroom pot pie. Additionally, drying it for later use prevents sponginess and worm infestation.

MEDICINAL USE: Used in traditional medicine for its antiviral, antibacterial, and antifungal effects.

HARVESTING: Optimal from summer to fall; choose young, fresh specimens with closed or just-opening caps; cut stipe at the base with a knife, avoiding damage to surrounding mycelium.

CAUTION: Cook thoroughly; avoid collecting from busy roadsides, and polluted areas due to potential cadmium accumulation.

POISONOUS LOOK-ALIKES: *Agaricus placomyces, Agaricus xanthodermus (page 114)*

• *A. augustus:* Strong almond-like odor, yellow staining on cap and base of stipe.

• *A. placomyces:* Phenolic or chemical odor, doesn't stain yellow, more robust appearance.

Agaricus placomyces

General Information

OTHER NAMES: Shaggy mane, lawyer's wig

SIZE: Cap 1.5-3 inches (4-8 cm) in diameter, stipe 2.5-16 inches (6-40 cm) tall

HABITATS: Grassy areas, meadows, parks, gardens, and disturbed ground, often found in clusters or lines along the edges of paths and roads

EDIBLE PARTS: Cap (only when young and fresh)

84 Shaggy Ink Cap
Coprinus comatus

IDENTIFICATION: This mushroom is unusual as it turns black and dissolves itself hours after being picked or depositing spores.

CAP: White, cylindrical to conical shape, featuring shaggy, pale brown scales concentrated on the top of the cap for added texture.

GILLS: Starting out as white, the gills transition to a pinkish hue and ultimately turn black as the mushroom matures. During this process, the gills dissolve into a black, spore-filled liquid, giving rise to the common name "ink cap."

STIPE: Exhibiting a white hue, the stipe has a smooth surface and may display a loose, delicate ring near the bottom.

FLESH: White.

SPORE PRINT: Black.

ODOR: Mild, mushroomy odor.

EDIBLE USE: Enjoy young and fresh, before gills blacken and auto-digest. Sauté, fry or incorporate into soups, stews, and omelets for a mild, delicate flavor. Cook promptly after harvesting due to rapid deterioration. To store, sauté or simmer until tender, cool, then transfer to airtight containers or freezer bags. Immersing freshly harvested mushrooms in a glass of ice water delays decomposition for a day or two, maintaining quality until ready to cook or process.

MEDICINAL USE: Contain antioxidants and bioactive compounds with potential health benefits.

HARVESTING: Best from later summer to fall; choose young specimens with white gills and intact cap scales; cut at the base of the stipe, preserving mycelium.

CAUTION: Consuming the mushroom followed by alcohol can trigger adverse effects, including facial flushing, palpitations, a metallic taste, nausea, and tingling sensations. In some cases, reactions may be more intense. To prevent these symptoms, it's recommended to avoid alcohol for several days both before and after consuming this mushroom.

85 King Bolete
Boletus edulis

OTHER NAMES: Cep, penny bun, porcino, porcini

SIZE: Cap 3-12 inches (8-30 cm) diameter, stipe 3-10 inches (8-25 cm) tall

HABITATS: Deciduous and coniferous forests, forming symbiotic relationships with trees such as pine, spruce, and oak

EDIBLE PARTS: The whole fruiting body

IDENTIFICATION FEATURES

CAP: Large, brown, convex when young and flattens with age; smooth or slightly cracked surface that may be sticky when wet.

TUBES: Distinct elongated structures beneath the cap, housing spores for dispersal; change from whitish to greenish-yellow as they mature; directly attached to the stipe.

PORES: Tube openings start as white, shift to yellow, then brown with age; do not stain when bruised.

STIPE: Bare, club-shaped; white or yellowish, solid and firm when young; with a raised network pattern called reticulation on its upper part.

FLESH: White, thick, and firm when young; turns spongy with age; does not change color when bruised or cut.

SPORE PRINT: Olive brown.

ODOR: Mild, pleasant, slightly sweet.

EDIBLE USE: Highly prized for a rich, nutty flavor and meaty texture. Versatile in various dishes, both fresh and dried. Fresh ones can be sautéed, grilled, or roasted for pasta, risotto, or stews. Dried ones, with a more concentrated flavor, are ideal for soups, sauces, risotto, and casseroles. Thick caps are suitable for slicing and frying or grilling, while diced stipes add depth to dishes. Pairs well with garlic, butter, and parsley, and complements traditional Italian recipes like tagliatelle al fungi or creamy mushroom risotto. Also works well in stir-fries, omelets, and quiches.

HARVESTING: Optimal in summer and fall. Choose firm, dry fruiting bodies free of worms or maggots. Cut the stipe at the base with a knife, clean with a brush or damp cloth, and discard damaged or rotten parts.

CAUTION: Cook thoroughly before eating; avoid consuming those exposed to pollution or pesticides.

POISONOUS LOOK-ALIKES: *Boletus edulis* has few poisonous look-alikes, which can be easily distinguished by examining the colors of pores, stipes, or smells.

OTHER NAMES: Rough-stemmed bolete, scaber stalk

SIZE: Cap 2-6 inches (5-15 cm) in diameter, stipe 2-6 inches (5-15 cm) tall

HABITATS: Commonly found in association with birch trees, often growing in mixed forests or near forest edges

EDIBLE PARTS: The whole fruiting body

86 Birch Bolete
Leccinum scabrum

IDENTIFICATION FEATURES

CAP: Large and dark brown, transitioning from convex to flat as it matures. The cap is dry, slightly rough, and smooth with a contrasting lighter edge.

PORES: Start off white, then change to a yellowish-brown hue. In older mushrooms, the pores may protrude on the cap and indent near the stipe. This pore layer can be easily separated from the cap skin.

STIPE: Slender, featuring a mix of white and dark to black flakes; lacks a ring.

FLESH: Whitish, sometimes darkening upon exposure, firm in young specimens, becomes spongy and water-absorbent, particularly in rainy weather. Does not change color when exposed to air.

SPORE PRINT: Brown to olive-brown.

ODOR: Mild and pleasant.

EDIBLE USE: The mushroom has a mild, earthy taste and a meaty texture. It can be sautéed, roasted, grilled, or added to soups, stews, risottos, and pasta dishes, pairing well with garlic, onions, and herbs. Its hearty texture also lends itself to being incorporated into savory pies or rich, robust pasta sauces.

However, it is crucial to cook the mushroom thoroughly before consumption to avoid gastrointestinal upset. Whether served with its dark, rough cap or prepared with a smoky taste from grilling, this mushroom adds depth and flavor to various dishes.

MEDICINAL USE: Known to be a good source of dietary fiber, vitamins, and minerals. It has potential antioxidant and anti-inflammatory properties.

HARVESTING: Optimal in late summer and fall, under birch trees; choose young, firm specimens; cut stipe at the base with a knife, and leave a small portion to avoid damaging mycelium.

CAUTION: Cook thoroughly to prevent gastrointestinal upset. Some individuals might still experience digestive discomfort after consuming, so it's essential to start with a small amount.

87 Beefsteak Mushroom

Fistulina hepatica

IDENTIFICATION FEATURES

CAP: Reddish-brown, tongue or kidney-shaped. The cap is thick, fleshy, and often has a moist and rough-textured surface.

TUBES: Cream to pinkish, elongated tubes

PORES: Small, irregular, crowded pores.

STIPE: Absent or rudimentary; cap usually attached directly to the tree.

FLESH: The flesh is firm, succulent, and juicy. Its deep red to maroon color is notable, and when squeezed, it exudes a red liquid.

SPORE PRINT: Pinkish-brown.

ODOR: Mild, somewhat sour.

EDIBLE USE: The mushroom offers a meaty texture and a tangy, slightly acidic flavor that pairs well with various cooking methods. Before cooking, marinate it in herbs and spices to enhance the taste. Grilling the mushroom like a steak imparts a charred, smoky flavor, while slicing it into strips makes it perfect for stir-fries, fajitas, or sautéed dishes. Young, tender caps can be used as a meat substitute in sandwiches, burgers, stroganoffs, and casseroles. For a different culinary approach, try

General Information

OTHER NAMES: Beefsteak fungus, ox tongue

SIZE: Cap 2.8-12 inches (7-30 cm) across, 0.8-2.5 inches (2-6 cm) thick

HABITATS: Growing on living or dead hardwoods, particularly oak, and chestnut

EDIBLE PARTS: Cap

incorporating it into a flavorful mushroom pâté or thinly slicing and adding it to a fresh salad. Younger mushrooms are ideal, as older ones may become tough and fibrous.

MEDICINAL USE: Anti-inflammatory and antioxidant properties; potential wound-healing and antiviral activities.

HARVESTING: Optimal in late summer and fall; harvest young, tender specimens; use a sharp knife to cut the cap from the tree without damaging the mycelium; clean by wiping with a damp cloth; avoid washing under water.

POISONOUS LOOK-ALIKES: No known toxic look-alikes, but some tough, inedible polypores may resemble beefsteak mushroom; check for the presence of elongated tubes and reddish flesh to confirm identification.

88 Chicken of the Woods

Laetiporus sulphureus

IDENTIFICATION: This mushroom has large, bright yellow to orange overlapping shelves, with a smooth, wavy top surface.

SHELVES: Fruiting body grows from the tree trunk, starting as a knob and expanding into fan-shaped shelves in overlapping tiers. Color ranges from sulfur-yellow to bright orange, with a suede-like texture. Old mushrooms fade to pale beige.

PORES: Small pores on the underside, sulfur-yellow spore-producing surface.

STIPE: No distinct ring or stipe present.

FLESH: Fresh is succulent, with a strong fungal aroma and yellowish juice, and becomes dry and brittle over time.

SPORE PRINT: White to pale yellow.

ODOR: Mild, pleasant.

EDIBLE USE: Valued as a meat substitute in various dishes, this mushroom offers a chicken-like flavor and texture. Best enjoyed when young and tender, it can be sautéed, roasted, or cooked in soups and stews. Pan-frying in butter or oil with garlic and herbs enhances

General Information

OTHER NAMES: Sulphur shelf

SIZE: Shelves up to 24 inches (60 cm) across

HABITATS: Grows on living or dead hardwood trees, such as oaks, beech, and cherry. It is usually found at the base of the trunk or on large branches

EDIBLE PARTS: Shelves (tender, outer edges of young specimens)

its taste. The tender texture and unique flavor make it a fantastic addition to stir-fries, tacos, or pasta. Pairing well with creamy sauces, it can also replace meat in dishes like chicken alfredo, pot pie, or curry.

MEDICINAL USE: It is believed to have anti-inflammatory and antioxidant properties. It has been used in traditional medicine for its potential anticancer and immune-boosting effects.

HARVESTING: Optimal in summer and fall; harvest young specimens with tender outer edges, as older portions tend to be tough and unpalatable; use a sharp knife and clean with a damp cloth.

CAUTION: Gastrointestinal upset is possible; try a small amount first to test tolerance.

OTHER NAMES: Bearded tooth mushroom, pom pom blanc

SIZE: 4-10 inches (10-25 cm) in diameter

HABITATS: Hardwood trees

EDIBLE PARTS: The whole fruiting body is edible

89 Lion's Mane
Hericium erinaceus

IDENTIFICATION: The lion's mane does not have the traditional mushroom cap, gills, or stipe like many other fungi. Instead, it's characterized by its unique appearance of cascading spines.

CAP: It lacks a traditional cap. Instead, it has a dense, unbranched, clump-like structure from which the spines cascade.

SPINES: Instead of gills, it has long, icicle-like spines (or "teeth") where the spores are produced. These spines are white to cream-colored, long (typically more than 0.4 inches or 1 cm in length), and droop from the main body, becoming more yellowish-brown with age or when bruised.

STIPE: The lion's mane lacks a defined stipe. The fungal body attaches directly to the wood substrate.

FLESH: White, soft, breaking apart easily.

SPORE PRINT: White.

ODOR: Pleasant and mushroom-like.

EDIBLE USE: Lion's mane mushroom is renowned for its culinary and medicinal properties. When cooked, the texture is reminiscent of seafood, like crab or lobster, making it a popular vegetarian substitute in various dishes. Its sweet and delicate flavor absorbs the flavors it is cooked with. It can be sauteed, baked, or stewed and is an excellent addition to soups, pasta, or stir-fries. Furthermore, it is also ground into powder and used as a nutritious addition to smoothies or health drinks.

MEDICINAL USE: The mushroom is revered in traditional medicine for its potential neuroprotective and nootropic effects. Research suggests it might boost cognitive function, help repair nerve damage, and reduce anxiety and depression.

HARVESTING: Lion's mane mushrooms are best harvested when they are young and all white. The spines should be firm and not releasing spores. Carefully cut at the base with a knife, leaving the substrate it is growing on undamaged to allow for future growth.

CAUTION: Some individuals may experience allergic reactions or mild digestive upset. It's advisable to start with small amounts and monitor for any adverse reactions.

90 The Deceiver
Laccaria laccata

IDENTIFICATION FEATURES

CAP: Can range in color from pinkish to brown, often changing with moisture and age. The cap has a striated margin and is initially convex but flattens with age.

GILLS: Broad, spaced, and attached to the stem. They range from pale pinkish to purple-brown.

STIPE: Slender, bare, 0.8-3.9 inches (2-10 cm) tall, and roughly the same color as the cap or slightly paler. It can be fibrous and is often slightly twisted.

FLESH: Thin and the same color as the cap.

SPORE PRINT: White.

ODOR: Mild and mushroomy.

EDIBLE USE: The deceiver is known for its mild, slightly sweet or nutty flavor and can be used in a variety of dishes. It is great in stews and soups, or sautéed with butter and garlic and served over pasta or on toast. It also complements meat dishes well. It can

be dried and stored for later use, adding a depth of flavor to winter dishes. While not a stand-out mushroom for taste, it's a reliable and versatile edible that can be used to bulk out foraged dishes.

HARVESTING: They fruit in the late summer to late autumn. Harvest younger, fresher specimens, as older ones can be tough and have a washed-out flavor.

POISONOUS LOOK-ALIKES: The deceiver has no deadly look-alikes, but it can be confused with other *Laccaria* species or small, brownish mushrooms. Always practice careful identification when foraging.

General Information

SIZE: 6-8 inches (15-20 cm) in diameter

HABITATS: Typically found in coniferous or mixed woods

EDIBLE PARTS: The entire mushroom is edible

91 Lobster Mushroom
Hypomyces lactifluorum

IDENTIFICATION: Lobster mushroom is a parasitic fungus that grows on certain species of mushrooms, notably *Russula* and *Lactarius*, altering their appearance dramatically. Here are the key identification features.

CAP: Bright orange to deep red, often deformed or irregular because it parasitizes other mushrooms. The original cap of the host mushroom becomes contorted and sometimes bumpy, often losing its original shape.

GILLS: The gills of the host mushroom get covered and are often not prominently visible. The parasitic overgrowth can obscure the original gill pattern.

STIPE: Like the cap, the stipe is also covered by the bright orange to reddish-orange parasitic layer. It may become more robust and may lose its original definition. The base can sometimes be bulbous.

SPORE PRINT: Spore print is rarely done as the parasitic layer makes it difficult.

ODOR: Distinctive and pleasant, reminiscent of seafood, especially cooked lobster or shrimp.

EDIBLE USE: Lobster mushrooms are valued for their dense, crunchy texture and seafood-like flavor. They can be used in any recipe that calls for mushrooms, but they particularly shine in dishes where their unique flavor and texture can be highlighted. For example, they can be sautéed with butter and garlic and served on toast, used as a pizza topping, or included in pasta dishes. They also pair well with eggs in an omelet or quiche. Because of their seafood-like flavor, they can also be used as a vegan substitute for lobster or crab in recipes.

HARVESTING: Lobster mushrooms are harvested in the late summer and fall. They are usually found partially emerging from the soil. To harvest, cut the mushroom at the base using a knife, leaving the underground parts undisturbed.

POISONOUS LOOK-ALIKES: Lobster mushrooms are relatively safe to forage because of their distinctive color and the fact that they parasitize other mushrooms, giving them a unique and identifiable shape. However, they can occasionally colonize inedible or mildly toxic mushroom species, so caution is advised.

OTHER NAMES: Maitake, ram's head, sheep's head

SIZE: Can grow to be very large, often 10 inches (25 cm) in height and up to several feet in width

HABITATS: At the base of hardwood trees, particularly oaks

EDIBLE PARTS: The whole fruiting body

92 Hen of the Woods
Grifola frondosa

IDENTIFICATION FEATURES

CAP: Multi-capped, with clusters of overlapping rosettes or fan-shaped fronds growing from a single, branched stem structure. Caps are grayish-brown to brown. Each individual cap is relatively small (3-10 cm), wavy, and often curled or spoon-shaped.

UNDERSIDE: White to pale gray pore surface instead of gills. The pores are tiny and can appear almost smooth.

STIPE: The mushroom has a branched, central, thick base from which the individual fronds emerge. This base can sometimes be buried within the leaf litter or substrate.

FLESH: Firm and fleshy, especially when young. As it matures, it becomes tougher and more fibrous.

SPORE PRINT: White to pale cream.

ODOR: Not distinctive when fresh but can have a pleasant mushroomy aroma when cooked.

EDIBLE USE: Hen of the woods is a very versatile mushroom when it comes to cooking. Its firm, chewy texture holds up well in soups, stews, and stir-fries, and its flavor is enhanced when paired with ingredients like garlic, thyme, and sage. Many people enjoy it simply sautéed in butter or olive oil. It can also be used as a meat substitute in various dishes due to its hearty texture. In Japan, it's often used in tempura and in stir-fries. Additionally, the mushroom can be dried and then rehydrated for use in various dishes.

MEDICINAL USE: Hen of the woods has been used in traditional medicine, particularly in Asia, for centuries. It's believed to boost the immune system and is also being studied for potential anti-cancer properties.

HARVESTING: Hen of the woods should be harvested in the fall when they are young and the edges of the caps are still curled under. They should be firm and not slimy or decaying.

SIZE: 2-6 inches (5-15 cm) tall

HABITATS: Burn sites, recently disturbed areas, and coniferous forests

EDIBLE PARTS: The whole fruiting body

93 Black Morel
Morchella elata

IDENTIFICATION: The black morel stands out in the mushroom world with its unmistakable honeycomb-like cap exhibiting dark ridges contrasted by lighter pits and a hollow stipe.

CAP: A rich, dark brown or black cap, featuring deep pits and pronounced ridges that form a honeycomb pattern. The cap is attached to the stipe at its base.

STIPE: White or cream-colored, the stipe is hollow and may present a smooth or slightly wrinkled texture.

FLESH: Whitish color that remains unchanged even when exposed to air.

SPORE PRINT: Pale yellow to cream.

ODOR: Mild and pleasant.

EDIBLE USE: This sought-after, flavorful mushroom has a rich, nutty taste that's perfect for enhancing dishes like creamy sauces, pasta, or sautéed in butter with garlic and shallots. Drying and rehydrating them can intensify the flavor even further.

MEDICINAL USE: Source of vitamins, minerals, and antioxidants. Have been used in traditional medicine for its antioxidant and immune-boosting properties.

HARVESTING: April to June in North America; found in coniferous and deciduous forests, often in areas affected by forest fires; avoid picking in polluted areas; use a knife to cut stipe at the base or gently twist off.

CAUTION: Always cook morels before eating, as raw specimens contain toxins that can cause gastrointestinal discomfort. Avoid collecting morels from potentially contaminated areas, such as those near roads or polluted water sources.

POISONOUS LOOK-ALIKES: The toxic false morel (*Gyromitra spp.*)

• True morels have a honeycomb cap, while false morels have a more irregular, brain-like, or wrinkled appearance.

• True morels have a cap attached directly to the stipe, creating a hollow chamber; false morels have a cap attached at the top, with the stipe potentially filled with cottony tissue.

Gyromitra spp.

General Information

OTHER NAMES: Bootlace fungus

SIZE: Cap 1-6 inches (3-15 cm) in diameter, stipe up to 8 inches (20 cm) tall

HABITATS: Grow in clusters at the base of trees, stumps, or on buried wood. They are parasitic and saprobic, often causing root rot in infected trees

EDIBLE PARTS: Cap and stipe (tough stipes are excluded)

94 Honey Fungus
Armillaria mellea

IDENTIFICATION FEATURES

CAP: Yellowish-brown to dark brown, convex to flat with age, slightly sticky surface when wet; margins arched at maturity.

GILLS: White to cream, wide apart, connect to stipe straight or slightly running down.

STIPE: Slender, narrowing towards the base; white at the top, brownish-yellow towards the bottom, with a dark base; initially has a firm, spongy, fibrillose consistency but later becomes hollow at maturity.

RING: Wide, soft-edged ring on stipe's upper part; white partial veil (protective covering) on young gills.

FLESH: White.

RHIZOMORPHS (MYCELIAL CORDS): Black, resembling shoelaces; primarily underground, sometimes above ground around the base of infected trees or on decaying wood.

SPORE PRINT: White.

ODOR: Mild and sweetish.

EDIBLE USE: Can be boiled and fried with butter and garlic, added to soups, stews, sauces, or casseroles for flavor and texture; can be dried and ground into a powder for seasoning or thickening, or pickled in vinegar and spices for later use. Stipe may be fibrous and tough, especially in older ones, so remove it before cooking. Parboiling can help remove any bitter taste.

MEDICINAL USE: Used in traditional medicine for its antioxidant, anti-inflammatory, and antimicrobial properties, by indigenous peoples as a laxative.

HARVESTING: Best in fall, when mushrooms grow around the base of infected trees; cut off at ground level with a sharp knife, avoiding dirt and debris.

CAUTION: Cook thoroughly to avoid gastrointestinal upset; honey mushrooms on certain tree species, such as eucalyptus, can be toxic.

POISONOUS LOOK-ALIKES: *Galerina marginata* (deadly poisonous) has the following features.

- Cap color: Brown to reddish-brown.
- Stipe: Light to dark brown.
- Habitats: Decaying wood or mossy logs.

Galerina marginata

95 Oyster Mushroom
Pleurotus ostreatus

IDENTIFICATION FEATURES

CAP: Smooth, moist, with a shape resembling an oyster or fan, usually in shades of white to gray or brown.

GILLS: White to cream-colored, descending the stem (if present). They are closely spaced.

STIPE: Usually short, eccentric to lateral (off-center), or sometimes absent. When present, it's thick and white.

FLESH: White, thick, and firm.

SPORE PRINT: White to lilac-gray.

ODOR: Mild, often described as bitter almond-like due to the presence of benzaldehyde.

EDIBLE USE: Oyster mushrooms are incredibly versatile in the kitchen, with a mild, slightly sweet flavor and soft texture that works well in a variety of dishes. They can be sautéed, grilled, braised, or stir-fried, and are a fantastic addition to soups, stews, and sauces. Oyster mushrooms also make a great base for vegetarian dishes due to their meaty texture. They pair well with many ingredients, from onions, garlic, and herbs to more robust flavors like soy sauce and sesame oil. They can be also used in making tempura or mixed with other vegetables for a healthy stir-fry.

MEDICINAL USE: Oyster mushrooms have been used in traditional medicine for their purported anti-inflammatory, antimicrobial, and antioxidant properties. Some research also suggests they may help lower cholesterol.

HARVESTING: Harvest oyster mushrooms when the edges of the caps are still curled downwards and the flesh is firm and not slimy or decaying.

POISONOUS LOOK-ALIKES: The poisonous *Omphalotus nidiformis*, or ghost fungus, looks similar but glows in the dark and has a much more bitter taste.

Omphalotus nidiformis

96 Dryad's Saddle
Polyporus squamosus

IDENTIFICATION FEATURES

CAP: Fan-shaped to almost round. Covered with dark brown, feathery scales on a cream to yellowish background.

PORES: Cream to pale yellow, round, and small; aging can lead them to become somewhat maze-like.

STIPE: Central or slightly off-center, thick, and can be short or long relative to the cap diameter. It's typically black and scaly at the base.

FLESH: Thick, white, soft in young specimens, but becoming tougher with age.

SPORE PRINT: White.

ODOR: Sweet, reminiscent of watermelon or cucumber.

EDIBLE USE: The dryad's saddle is a mushroom with a distinctive flavor, somewhat like cucumber or watermelon rind. Its texture is also unique, rather like a tender meat when it is young and fresh. Therefore, it can make a great substitute for meat in vegetarian dishes.

General Information

OTHER NAMES: Pheasant's back mushroom

SIZE: Can grow quite large, with caps often reaching 12 inches (30 cm) in diameter

HABITATS: Primarily on dead hardwoods, particularly on logs, stumps, and trunks

EDIBLE PARTS: Younger, tender parts of the cap and the edges

It works well in soups and stews, adding a depth of flavor and an interesting texture. It can be fried, sautéed, or grilled, and pairs well with hearty flavors such as garlic, onion, and rich sauces. The key to the best culinary use is to harvest it young and to cook it thoroughly to soften the texture.

MEDICINAL USE: While not commonly used for medicinal purposes, some studies suggest potential antioxidant and anti-inflammatory properties.

HARVESTING: Harvest younger specimens, as they become tough and leathery with age. Look for them in spring and early summer.

97 Saffron Milk Cap
Lactarius deliciosus

OTHER NAMES: Red pine mushroom

SIZE: Cap 1.5-5 inches (4-13 cm) in diameter, stipe 1-3 inches (3-8 cm) tall

HABITATS: Coniferous and mixed forests, forms mycorrhizal relationships with various pine species

EDIBLE PARTS: The whole fruiting body

IDENTIFICATION FEATURES

CAP: Starts as convex to vase-shaped but becomes flat or slightly depressed with age. Its color ranges from orange to red-orange with concentric circles of darker shades. The cap is smooth and can be sticky when wet, but it dries in dry weather. Notably, it turns green when bruised or exposed to air.

GILLS: Crowded, attached to stipe or slightly descending. Color ranges from pinkish tan to orange. When damaged, they exude a bright orange latex that stains green.

STIPE: Bare, cylindrical, often hollow; same color as the cap with darker orange spots.

FLESH: White to pale orange; releases orange latex that doesn't change color when cut or bruised.

SPORE PRINT: Pale yellow to buff.

ODOR: Mild and pleasant.

EDIBLE USE: It has a mild, slightly nutty flavor and is popular in Spain and Portugal cuisines. Common preparation methods include grilling, frying, baking, or stewing. It pairs well with onions, garlic, tomatoes, and herbs. It's a staple in traditional dishes like migas and arroz con setas and can be added to pasta, risotto, and omelets. Cooking it long and slow can enhance its naturally grainy texture. For preservation, pickling or salting works well, , providing a unique flavor to various dishes throughout the year.

HARVESTING: Found individually or in groups, often forming rings or arcs; best harvested late summer to mid-winter; cut stipe at the base with a knife, leaving the small part in the ground to minimize disturbance to mycelium.

CAUTION: It may cause allergic reactions in some people; don't eat too much at once as it may cause urine to turn orange or red due to pigments.

POISONOUS LOOK-ALIKES: *Lactarius torminosus* (toxic)

• *L. deliciosus*: Orange cap, orange milk, greenish staining on bruised areas.

• *L. torminosus*: Pinkish-orange cap, white milk, no green staining, cap margin with woolly hairs (hairy or wool-like appearance).

Lactarius torminosus

OTHER NAMES: Blue russula

SIZE: Cap 1.5-7 inches (4-18 cm) in diameter, stipe 2.5-4.5 inches (6-12 cm) tall

HABITATS: Found most commonly in beech forests, and often in deciduous or mixed forests

EDIBLE PARTS: The whole fruiting body

98 Charcoal Burner
Russula cyanoxantha

IDENTIFICATION: The most distinct features are gills that do not split, and the green reaction of the stipe when rubbed with iron salts (ferrous sulphate).

CAP: The cap begins as a convex shape, later flattening out as it matures, varying from purple to violet to blue in color. Cap color can fade with age or exposure to sunlight, becoming grayish or brownish. Cap color can also change when bruised, turning pinkish or reddish in some areas.

GILLS: Attached and crowded, white to cream in color. Gills feel greasy, flexible, and don't break easily.

STIPE: White, without a ring. It turns green when rubbed with iron salts (ferrous sulphate), unlike most other Russula species, which turn salmon.

SPORE PRINT: white to cream.

ODOR: Mild, nutty.

FLESH: White.

EDIBLE USE: Considered a prized addition to any gourmet dish, this mushroom has a mild, nutty flavor and a soft, greasy texture. It can be sautéed, grilled, or used in various dishes like pasta sauces, salads, scrambled eggs, pies, or soups. Its texture holds up well to cooking, making it a great addition to stir-fries, casseroles, and even a topping on gourmet pizzas. It can also be pickled, salted, or dried for preservation.

HARVESTING: Best from mid-summer to late fall. Choose young specimens with firm flesh. Use a knife to cut the stipe at the base, leaving a small portion to avoid damaging the mycelium.

CAUTION: When harvesting the charcoal burner, ensure proper identification as many *Russula* species look similar and some can be inedible or cause gastrointestinal upset. Thorough cooking is recommended to mitigate potential irritants. Always consume a small amount first to check for individual sensitivities and avoid mixing with other wild foods to trace any adverse reactions.

99 Weeping Bolete
Suillus granulatus

IDENTIFICATION FEATURES

CAP: Convex to flat. Cap color ranges from yellow-brown to reddish-brown, sticky when wet, and shiny when dry.

PORES: Small, pale yellow, exude pale milky droplets when young.

STIPE: Cylindrical, white to cream in color, and covered with tiny brownish granules at the top of the stipe. Does not have a ring.

SPORE PRINT: Brownish-yellow.

ODOR: Mild and earthy.

FLESH: Pale yellow.

EDIBLE USE: The weeping bolete is a versatile ingredient used in various dishes, offering a mild, earthy flavor that complements many ingredients. It's commonly used in soups, stews, and sauces, and its unique texture makes it suitable for stir-fries and pasta dishes. Enhance its flavor by sautéing it in butter or oil with garlic and herbs. However, like all Suillus species, the cap skin and tube layer are recommended to be removed prior to cooking, leaving behind only the firm flesh of the cap for culinary use. This practice improves the texture and overall mouthfeel of

General Information

OTHER NAMES: Granulated bolete

SIZE: Cap 1.5-4.5 inches (4-12 cm) in diameter, stipe 1.5-3 inches (4-8 cm) tall

HABITATS: Forms mycorrhizal associations with pine trees and is commonly found in coniferous forests and pine plantations

EDIBLE PARTS: Cap

the prepared mushroom.

HARVESTING: It's best to harvest in summer and fall within coniferous forests, especially under pine trees. Opt for young and firm specimens with unopened or freshly opened caps. To harvest, either cut at the base of the stipe or twist them gently to remove them from the ground.

CAUTION: Cook thoroughly before consuming. While it may cause gastrointestinal discomfort, removing the slimy cap skin can enhance its texture and taste.

POISONOUS LOOK-ALIKES: The mushroom can be confused with other *Suillus* species, but most are considered edible or, at worst, cause mild gastrointestinal issues. Examining the stipe granules, cap color, and habitat can help differentiate weeping bolete from look-alikes.

General Information

OTHER NAMES: Aniseed funnel

SIZE: Cap 1-3 inches (3-8 cm) in diameter, stipe 1.5-2.5 inches (4-6 cm) tall

HABITATS: Near deciduous and coniferous trees

EDIBLE PARTS: The whole fruiting body

100 Aniseed Toadstool
Clitocybe odora

IDENTIFICATION FEATURES

CAP: Convex to flat cap that becomes funnel-shaped with age. The cap is blue-green to greenish-gray and smooth. Young specimens have light blue caps, which fade to gray as they mature.

GILLS: Displaying a white to pale cream color, gills extend downward, attach to the stipe, and are closely spaced.

STIPE: Thick, white to pale blue-green; smooth and cylindrical. The stipe is attached to the gills without any rings.

FLESH: White to pale blue-green in color.

SPORE PRINT: White to cream.

ODOR: Strong aniseed-like aroma.

EDIBLE USE: Known for its distinctive anise-like aroma, this mushroom is a delightful flavor enhancer in various dishes. It can be used fresh in salads, sautéed with butter and garlic, or added to soups, stews, and pasta sauces. It's also popular for flavoring mushroom pâtés or incorporated into a creamy, fragrant risotto. Additionally, its unique fragrance lends itself well to desserts like anise-flavored cookies or as a garnish for sweet dishes.

HARVESTING: Collect mature mushrooms with a strong aniseed scent from mid-summer to early winter. Cut the stipe at the base, ensuring the mycelium remains undisturbed.

Avoid young specimens to prevent confusion with similar poisonous species.

POISONOUS LOOK-ALIKES: Steer clear of young mushrooms, as they can be mistaken for the toxic *Stropharia aeruginosa*. For fully grown specimens, the distinct aniseed aroma helps differentiate them from potentially harmful look-alikes.

Stropharia aeruginosa

RESOURCES

Here are some resources that North American foragers may find useful:

Books

Invest in field guides specific to your region that focus on plant identification. Field guides, such as the "Peterson Field Guide to Medicinal Plants and Herbs" or the "National Audubon Society Field Guide to North American Wildflowers," provide detailed information on plant identification, habitat, and range. What's more, "The Forager's Harvest" by Samuel Thayer is widely appreciated for its practical insights and detailed information.

Field guides focusing on North American mushrooms, such as "Mushrooms and Other Fungi of North America" by Roger Phillips or "National Audubon Society Field Guide to North American Mushrooms" by Gary H. Lincoff, are helpful resources for identifying and learning about mushrooms. These guides often provide information on habitat, edibility, and other relevant details.

Online resources

There are several online databases dedicated to plant information, such as the USDA PLANTS Database (https://plants.sc.egov.usda.gov/) and the Lady Bird Johnson Wildflower Center's Native Plant Database (https://www.wildflower.org/plants/).

Additionally, you can explore iNaturalist (https://www.inaturalist.org/), a community-based platform where people share their observations of plants and animals. By searching for a specific plant species, you can see when and where other users have observed it, which can give you a better understanding of its phenology in different regions.

Mushroom Observer (https://mushroomobserver.org): Mushroom Observer is a collaborative platform for recording, sharing, and discussing observations of mushrooms. You can search for specific species or browse by location to learn more about the mushrooms found in North America.

Local workshops and classes

Many areas have local experts who organize foraging workshops and guided walks. Check with your local parks, nature centers, or meetup groups to see if any events are available in your area.

Engaging with a community of fellow foragers can be incredibly enriching. Look for local foraging groups on social media platforms or in your community.

Remember, while these resources are incredibly helpful, nothing can replace the value of personal experience. Each foraging expedition is an opportunity to learn, grow, and hone your skills. So, use these resources as tools to guide your journey, not as a replacement for the journey itself.

Finally, look forward to our upcoming books that will delve even deeper into the realm of natural foods and self-sufficiency. We will provide more insights and guidance on how to live sustainably and harmoniously with nature.

Happy foraging, and remember, the most essential tool in your foraging kit is your sense of curiosity and wonder. Keep that alive, and the wild will always have treasures to reveal.

INDEX

PHOTOGRAPHY CREDITS

Made in the USA
Coppell, TX
01 February 2024

28479145R00077